Beate C. Kirchner

111 Places in Florence and Northern Tuscany That You Must Not Miss

Photographs by Francesco P. Carbone

D1547039

emons:

© Emons Verlag GmbH
All rights reserved
Edited by Katrina Fried
Design: Eva Kraskes, based on a design
by Lübbeke | Naumann | Thoben
Maps: altancicek.design, www.altancicek.de
English translation: Alan Gentile
Printing and binding: Grafisches Centrum Cuno, Calbe
Printed in Germany 2015
ISBN 978-3-95451-613-1
First edition

Did you enjoy it? Do you want more?
Join us in uncovering new places around the world on:
www.111places.com

Foreword

Classical cities of art, picturesque avenues lined with cypresses, magnificent pasta dishes, and full-bodied Chianti atop the table – these are the images that come to mind when we think of Tuscany. And it really is that beautiful just about everywhere you look. But who among us also conjures up visions of an alpine pasture that clings to the mountainside more than 3,000 feet up? Or knows about the largest marshland in Italy? And who has heard about the sparkly white "Caribbean beaches"?

This book guides you to 111 surprising places in nature and the art world, through their moving histories, bizarre stories, and curious personalities. Discover the village of Gallicano, where cheese throwers gather for their official championship; or Vicopisano, where you can view five centuries of prison graffiti. Visit the places that once filled the headlines of tabloids, like the Villa Varramsita, where offspring of the Agnelli family, who founded FIAT, lived and loved.

Explore those curiosities often missed even by the locals. Learn about the *buchette del vino*, the first roadside taverns of the Middle Ages; the city's oldest meteorological station at the Mercato San Lorenzo; and the pirate flags that decorate the church of Santo Stefano dei Cavalieri in Pisa. Discover high-caliber art that's off the beaten track: a marble pulpit where Dante gave some of his most moving speeches in the small church of San Leonardo in Arcetri; and a Madonna by Botticelli, the creator of the famous *Birth of Venus*, in Settignano, which you can admire without interruption. And finally, relish the classics of the Northern Italian kitchen: savor the black salami of Giustagnana and the wine from Pietrasanta, whose taste hints of the sea.

Here is Tuscany as you never knew it existed and always dreamt it would be.

111 Places

1 Monte Giovi

Summit atop the summit

On the summit of Monte Giovi, rebels formed partisan brigades towards the end of World War II as part of a resistance movement against the German occupation. The site was crucial for its strategic position, so close to Florence and lying at an altitude of 3,200 feet, where volunteers from the surrounding towns came together. The resistance fighters were welcomed in the countryside enclaves. Whole villages, such as Acone, offered the partisans accommodations, and in return the resistance fighters defended the crops of the farmers.

To commemorate the founding of the brigades, a stone pyramid was erected, which is adorned once a year with the Italian flag. Since 1949, a memorial celebration has been held atop the mountain on the second weekend in July. Young people often camp out and celebrate by eating, drinking, and partying.

But this is a remarkable place every day of the year. From the top of the mountain you can see in one direction over the Sieve valley, and in another the green valley of the Mugello. There is a small lake that offers refreshment in summer.

The fish from the lake are often served at the mountain lodge called Bottega di Monte Giovi, where they are prepared "homestyle"; same with the wild boar, which is supplied by hunters of the area. The mushrooms for the risotto also come from the surrounding wooded hills. Don't miss the *tortelli di patate mugellari*, a pasta specialty of the region. In the Bottega di Monte Giovi, everything is simple and original, and from the terrace you can look out over the lush countryside. It is open every day, and those wishing to spend the night can cheaply rent one of six guest rooms. Visitors arriving on horseback can also lodge their animals in the barn. The married couple that serves as your hosts are happily retired here – it is a beautiful place!

Address Via Palagio in Colognole 74, 50065 Pontassieve | Getting there From Florence take SS 67 toward Pontassieve, then continue toward Rufina and on to Scopertina. Take the exit for Colognole and turn left along the Sieve until you see the sign for La Bottega di Monte Giovi. Continue on for another mile or so along the unpaved road. | Tip There are many beautiful hiking trails where you can follow in the footsteps of the partisans, for example from Dicomano to the CAI 11 (visit www.cai.it).

2__ The Hospital of the Knights of Tau

An emergency room from the Middle Ages

Altopascio sits along the most dangerous stretch (from Pavia to Rome) of the Via Francigena, the only road that connected the north and the south in the early Middle Ages. The Arno River regularly overflowed its banks here, a boggy marsh filled the lowlands, and summertime was full of the threat of malaria.

For pilgrims and other travelers, the chiming of the bells in the tower of the hospital signified the only landmark after nightfall. The hospital door was always open, and pilgrims were given meals, either of wine and meat or of bread and water, depending on their social status. The hospital was associated with the Order of St. James of Altopascio, one of the oldest chivalric orders in Europe. They were also known as the Knights of the Tau, for the T-shaped cross adorning their clothing. The hospital was well equipped, and had a medical herb garden and a staff who could perform surgical procedures.

The Knights of the Tau were compassionate and extremely enterprising. They maintained roads and were responsible for bridge construction. Not just pilgrims, but also merchants and shepherds wanted a shortcut at a convenient crossing over the River Arno. They were forced to pay a toll, however – a lucrative business for the Knights of the Tau: in the middle of the 13th century the hospital was the richest religious institution in the entire diocese of Lucca.

In the late Middle Ages, the hospital lost some of its stature when the marshes were drained and it temporarily became an agricultural enterprise. It eventually closed in 1773. It is a nice walk along the old walls and across the Piazza degli Ospitalieri, and also worth a visit to the museum, where you can learn about the hospital's history.

Address Piazza degli Ospitalieri 6, 55011 Altopascio | Getting there From Lucca, drive about 12.5 miles on E 76 to the Altopascio exit. From Florence, about 37 miles on E 76. | Tip Bread in Altopascio is considered a particular specialty. Be sure to try a bit of focaccia while you're there. In May, during the celebration of the *festa del pane*, you can sample several different varieties.

3_ The Via Francigena
On the pilgrimage trail

It is said that, "A pilgrimage is the way of the soul through the maze of life," but this particular maze is a doozy. Cartography in the Middle Ages touched on the vague notion that Jerusalem sat in the center of the world – the place that would ultimately bring salvation to the planet. And in order to achieve salvation, a pilgrim had to face danger. He had to leave the familiar and the safe, and along the way meet devils, demons, and ghosts, which today might be referred to as storms, floods, or disease.

The Via Francigena, one of the oldest routes from the north of Europe to the south, led from Canterbury to Rome across France, through the Grand St. Bernard Pass and the Aosta Valley, through Piacenza in the Apennines and Siena in Tuscany. Comparing sources and the many descriptions of the path from ancient times, it becomes quickly apparent that a single Via Francigena did not exist. It was a series of old trunk roads that pilgrims used on their way to Rome to visit the tombs of the apostles Peter and Paul. It was often also referred to as the *Via Romea*, after its final destination.

The reconstruction of the Via Francigena today is based primarily on data from Sigerich, the Archbishop of Canterbury, who made the pilgrimage to Rome in 990. The old trail would likely have been completely lost to the ages if the Council of Europe had not declared it as a "Major Cultural Route" in 1994, at the request of the Italian government. The entire 1200-mile journey from Canterbury to Rome takes about three months to walk, and passes through a variety of terrains and weather conditions.

As signs point out today, you can begin a hike on the only known original section of the Via Francigena just several miles outside of the center of the town of Altopascio. This part of the pathway, with its large stones, leads magically through a small forest where a small church stands across a bridge – it's well worth a visit.

Address Via Ponticelli 249, 50054 Galleno | Getting there From Altopascio, head in the direction of Fucecchio. After the Chimenti neighborhood there is a rest stop with trees, two benches, and a sign reading *Tratto originale della Francigena*; from here, drive about 2.5 miles, or take the footpath over Villa Campanile. | Tip Altopascio is still a pilgrimage station today. With a credential (pilgrim's passport), you can get a stamp and a lodging allocation in the library at Piazza Cavalieri.

4 Hostel Antico Spedale
For pilgrims of the third millennium

"On the steep old road that leads to Arezzo, before coming to the house of Apparita, a grandiose and mighty building appears before you." These were the words the historian Guido Carocci (1851–1916) used to describe the Antico Spedale del Bigallo. Founded on the initiative of the rich Florentine Dioticidiede di Bonaguida del Dado, the place was earlier referred to as *Fonteviva* (literally "clear spring") because it lay close to the spring that was the monastery's water source, and thus supplied the weary travelers along the old pilgrimage route. Its current name comes from Compagnia del Bigallo, a brotherhood to defend the faith founded in the 13th century. Its coat of arms is clearly visible and appropriately depicts a rooster, or *gallo*.

After 1500, the complex was a cloistered convent for nuns who cared for the sick. The hospice was separated from the nuns' building and the garden, however, by high walls, which are still visible today. In 1808, the monastery was closed by the French and used as housing for many farming families. The town of Bagno a Ripoli bought the building in 1920 and eventually sheltered refugees there in the wake of World War II, after which the ex-convent stood vacant for a long period.

Beginning in the 1990s, the building was lovingly restored and expanded into a hostel. In the 15th-century Maria del Fonte chapel, white stucco works and ceiling paintings were brought back to life. The view of Florence from the terrace is enchanting, and the rooms are simple with a special, peaceful ambiance.

The Antico Spedale del Bigallo now caters to the pilgrims of the third millennium "who want to immerse themselves in an atmosphere outside of time and space, close to nature." It is in this vein that the cooperative of young people who manage the hostel today preach sustainable tourism.

Address Via del Bigallo e Apparita, 50012 Bagno a Ripoli, www.anticospedalebigallo.it |
Getting there Take A1 to the Firenze Sud exit. From there, follow the SP 127 toward
Florence and follow signs for Bagno a Ripoli. Next follow the brown signs through the
town to Antico Spedale Bigallo, which lies on the left about 1.5 miles after a curve. | Hours
Open Apr 1 – Sep 30 | Tip Tours through the beautiful surroundings are offered both on
foot and on horseback

5 Santa Caterina delle Ruote

Fresco frenzy

This idyllic location could not be more peaceful: in the midst of the green landscape on the edge of the Chianti region stands a modest church from the middle of the 14th century. The famous Alberti family, who originally commissioned the building, lived nearby in a country house with the name *Paradiso degli Alberti*. At first sight you will understand why the church, which has been deconsecrated, is often booked as a wedding venue.

From the outside, the building looks so simple and humble, and yet its interior is opulently decorated. As you enter, fireworks of colors and images explode before your eyes – a real rush for the senses. Paintings completely cover the walls and ceilings, right up to the pointed Gothic arches. The frescoes were restored a few years back and their bright colors once again shine. The artists who created the works were the Master of Barberino, Pietro Nelli, and Spinello Aretino. It is not easy to orient yourself among the wealth of imagery.

The frescoes depict the story of the martyr Catherine of Alexandria, who was sentenced to death in Alexandria for her Christian faith during the reign of the Roman emperor Maxentius (306–312). Before her execution, the highly educated woman was given the opportunity to repent and be converted to paganism by 50 scholars. Not only could they not dissuade her, but instead she converted *them* to Christianity. The emperor thus sent them all to the stake. Catherine herself was sentenced to death via the torture device of the wheel – hence the name *delle ruote*, or "of the wheels." Four wheels lined "with iron saws and sharp nails" were to tear at the unwavering martyr's flesh, but the device broke the minute it touched her. She was finally beheaded with a sword.

Address Via Del Carota, 50012 Bagno a Ripoli | **Getting there** Bus 31, 32 from Piazza San Marco to the Chiantigiana 7 stop. From there, on foot, take the road about 165 feet back to the Via Ferrero, turn right to Piazza Bacci, and follow signs to Santa Caterina delle Route, past the homes and the tennis courts to the sign for Ponte a Ema, then a slight right turn to the church (about 20 minutes). | **Hours** By appointment. Call Roberta Tucci, Tel +39/3355428515, and meet at the bus stop at Chiantigiana 7 | **Tip** Farther along the road, the landscape is unbelievably beautiful for a walk, and after a few miles you'll reach the Antico Ospedale del Bigallo along the Via Roma.

6_ The Whale Bone
When the Mugello was underwater

Along the road that leads to the famous Medici Villa in Cafaggiolo, it's worth making a short stop here, at a building that formerly housed the post office but now stands empty. Nobody would take any interest in it were it not for the crooked wooden-looking thing hanging on the wall under the roof.

In reality, it is a prehistoric whale bone; or more precisely, the tooth of a sperm whale measuring more than six and a half feet long. Exactly where it came from is unknown. The entire region, however, like the majority of Tuscany, was once underwater.

Up until 30 million years ago, this area where the Italian peninsula now stands was open ocean. Over the course of millions of years, land was formed through the sedimentation of soil. A small part of the sea became separated and formed a body of water, similar to an alpine lake, with a surface area of more than 77 square miles. Investigations of the sequence of layers of sedimentary rocks in the Mugello testify to this, along with a complete whale skeleton now on exhibition at the Museum of Mineralogy and Paleontology in Scandicci. The whale tooth is said to have come from one of the whales that once swam here in Mugello.

The bizarre maritime relic was not always displayed at the former post office. In a painting by Giusto Utens, an Italian painter of Flemish origin, which depicts the Medici Villa in Cafaggiolo in the year 1600, the whale bone is easily recognizable on one of the buildings. When a bourgeois family acquired the property from the royal family of Savoy in the second half of the 19th century, the bone was moved to its current location.

The water of the past has long since disappeared, but in its place nearby is a reservoir, the Lago di Bilancino. There you can take a dip during the hot summer months, and enjoy windsurfing, canoeing, and sailing.

Address Via Nazionale 16, 50031 Barberino di Mugello | Getting there From Florence, take A 1 to the Barberino di Mugello exit. At the roundabout take the third exit (Via del Lago), then at the next roundabout take the second exit (Via Nazionale), and keep right. | Tip In the Osteria Girodibacco at Via Nazionale 8 (www.girodibacco.it), the classic Florentine T-bone steak and hulled-wheat pasta with Pecorino cream is served alongside fresh mushrooms.

7 — Cathedral of San Christoforo

A mysterious inscription

Barga is picturesquely situated on a slope in the middle of the region formally known as Garfagnana. The Romanesque Cathedral of San Christoforo is perched high above the town: the view over the valley spreads wide in all directions across to the mountains, including Monte Forato, which on a clear day is said to look like a sleeping giant in the distance. The cathedral, with its simple facade, was constructed out of white limestone between the 12th and 14th centuries.

If you look closely, you'll see a hieroglyphic inscription at the entrance. It consists of Greek and Latin letters as well as other characters of uncertain origin. The enigmatic inscription has lured many illustrious personalities to the site, including Pope Paul III and Kaiser Karl V. But experts and researchers have never reached a consensus as to who created the inscription or what it means.

The philologist Augusto Mancini came to the conclusion in the 1950s that the characters are a clear reference to the Holy Trinity. A respected specialist in epigraphy (the study of ancient inscriptions) claims, however, that the correct transcription "Mi-cha-el" must be in reference to the archangel Michael, who leads the struggle between good and evil. Still other scientists believe the writing is Arabic. Another theory is that the Pope Alexander II created the engraving himself to commemorate his ordination. Or it could even have been the Fratelli Comacini, the builders union from Lombardy, who were supposedly later involved with the Freemasons, an allegation that is now vehemently denied.

The exact same inscription exists to the left of the entrance at the baptistery in Pisa as well as at the Church of San Frediano. The message, however, remains a mystery to this day.

Address Via del Pretorio, 55051 Barga | Getting there From Lucca, take SS 12 and SP 20 in the direction of Castelnuovo Garfagnana for about 30 miles. At the intersection in the town of Gallicano, turn right and follow the signs for Barga. | Tip Every year the Barga Jazz Festival is held in town (www.bargajazz.it).

8_ The Castle of Calenzano Alto

A small fortress with miniature soldiers

Those traveling from Florence toward Calenzano are usually on the hunt for bargains or designer clothes at the outlets. The area is characterized by large malls and bulky concrete buildings. But travel a few miles north into the hills and you will be led on a journey back to the Middle Ages.

Calenzano Alto today is still surrounded by its historic walls. The views into the valley spread in all four directions. The village, with its castle, is typical of the old fortified settlements nestled among the hills. From a height of over 650 feet, the castle controlled the major transport routes of the region, which joined the lowlands of Florence with the Mugello. During the Middle Ages, the border between the dioceses of Florence and Pistoia ran right through here. By the 13th century, Florence had taken control of the area and used Calenzano and the strategic valley as the access point for the plain of the Arno River.

Nearly everything in and around the castle looks the same as it did then: there are the two entrance gates, the piazza, the Palazzo del Podestà, the church of San Niccolò, and the narrow streets. A walk through the medieval alleys is full of ambiance, and when the humidity of the hot days in the city lingers on into the evenings, a cool breeze blows here.

On weekends, families come to visit the Museo del Figurino Storico (Museum of the Toy Soldier and Historic Figures), the only one of its kind in Italy, with exhibits from private collections in collaboration with the University of Siena. The museum offers a journey through history, from the Etruscans to the Romans to the wars of Napoleon's time. The section on World War II pays special homage to the Gothic Line and the resistance.

Address Via del Castello 7, 50041 Calenzano Alto | **Getting there** Take A 1 to the exit for Calenzano-Sesto Fiorentino. Continue toward Calenzano / Sesto Fiorentino, slightly to the left, then at the roundabout take the first exit, for Via Vittorio Emanuele. Take a right on Via del Garille, then at the next roundabout take the first exit, for Via S. Pertini, and at the next roundabout take the third exit, for Via Giuseppe Giusti. At the first intersection, take a left on Via Giacomo Puccini, then stay slightly right. | **Hours** Museum: Mon–Fri 4–7:30pm, Sat and Sun 10am–12pm and 4–7:30pm | **Tip** Gourmet cuisine is served with valley views at the Ristorante La Terrazza (Tel +39/0558873302).

9 __ Church of the Freeway

Service area for the faithful

The Church of the Freeway, or San Giovanni Battista, is widely visible from the southbound lanes of the highway in the hills at the northern end of Florence, yet few stop there even though the architect sought to entice them through his adventurous design.

The unusual church was built in 1960, and the commission came from the company that built the highway between Milan and Rome in the 1950s. The road – a classic symbol of the aspirations of Italy after the Second World War – had cost the lives of hundreds of workers, and thus it was determined that a monument should be built in their honor.

The dynamics of movement and travel provided the inspiration for the architect Giovanni Michelucci (1891 – 1990) – an outstanding representative of the avant-garde Gruppo Toscano school of architecture – who was instrumental in, among other things, the construction of the main railway station of Florence.

The church was built in the shape of a tent, where travelers find protection both in the literal and the spiritual sense. The eaves seem on the one hand to be in motion, and on the other hand are anchored firmly in the ground. Although the sails of the roof are made of concrete, they appear light and airy.

On the inside, there is a recurring motif of pathways. Beyond the entrance, a path lined with bronze reliefs runs parallel to the nave. Above the altar is a bright window with a modern representation of Jesus made out of iron bars and pieces of glass, reminiscent of a crown of thorns or barbed wire.

"The Church of the Freeway represents the high point in Michelucci's polemicizing criticism against the formal 'pleasing' (*piacevolezza*) of architecture," reads the subject literature. A stop on the highway offers an almost perfect opportunity to view the work of this great architect.

Address Via di Limite, 50013 Campi Bisenzio | Getting there From Florence, take the Peretola / Firenze-Mare highway, follow signs for Firenze Norte / A 1, and then follow signs for Chiesa di San Giovanni Battista. | Hours Mon – Sat 9am – 4:30pm, Sun 9am – 1pm and 3 – 6:30pm | Tip The Museum of Sacral Art, with works from the 16th century, is in San Donnino (open Fri 3:30 – 6pm, 2nd Sat of the month 4 – 6pm, Sun 9:30am – 12pm).

10__ The Hermitage of San Viano

The most beautiful alpine pasture in Tuscany

In Campocatino, you can stand at what feels like the end of the world. Some 30 small stone houses with crooked doors and windows and slate tiles on their roofs were built here in the Apuan Alps at an altitude of 3,280 feet. Originally, shepherds spent summers in these cottages with their sheep. It is a very peaceful place.

The romantic cottages – today all renovated with top-notch fixtures – now serve as weekend homes. Especially in August, evenings are enjoyed with cookouts in the fresh air. Fruit trees and elderberry bushes grow in the gardens. From here, the view out to Vagli Sotto into the valley is stunning. With luck, if you ask, the staff in the pub will rent you a *rifugio*, a place to spend the night in one of the stone huts, for a moderate price.

If not, you can borrow the key to the *eremo* – the hermitage of San Viano – from the bar and undertake the approximately 40-minute hike (sure-footedness needed) to the most beautiful alpine pasture in Tuscany. The location must truly have looked like the end of the world to Viano, who retired here in the 16th century. The pathway from Campocatino leads over the moraine hills of a glacier, through birch forests, and under cliffs to the pasture, which literally clings to the rock face of Monte Roccandagia, at 3,576 feet. It is said that Viano survived here by eating the wild herbs that grow on the barren rock walls.

When Viano died, the residents of Vagli declared him a saint. Since then, Beato Viano has been considered the patron saint of the shepherds, and is commemorated annually on the 2nd Sunday in June with the procession of a statue, which remains in the church in Campotino until September, the same amount of time that the shepherds used to stay in the mountains.

Address Loc. Campocatino, 55030 Vagli Sotto | **Getting there** From Vagli Sotto, head in the direction of Vagli Sopra. From there, follow the signs along the winding road to Campocatino. | **Tip** At Agriturismo Mulin del Rancone (www.mulindelrancone.com), about 30 minutes from Campocatino, you can stay in an old mill by a stream with riding stables and a restaurant that serves products from the farm.

11__The Gaetano Bresci Memorial

The assassin becomes the hero

In May 1898, the price of grain rose from the equivalent of 35 cents to 60 cents per kilo. This provoked the "Protest of the Stomach" in Milan. King Umberto I called a state of emergency and appointed General Fiorenzo Bava Beccaris as commander of the city garrisons.

At a protest rally, Bava Beccaris ordered soldiers to fire on the unarmed demonstrators, and 200 people were killed. The old general was scorned by the public as a brutal butcher and the incident came to be known as the "Massacre of Milan." Umberto I, however, thanked Beccaris for his courageous defense of the royal palace. He received the Great Cross of the Order of Savoy in June 1898 and was appointed to the Italian Senate.

News of this soon reached the anarchist Gaetano Bresci, who was working in the fabric industry in New Jersey. Bresci packed a bag, crossed the ocean, and on July 29, 1900, fired three shots at King Umberto I, killing the monarch as he rode in his car past the park of Villa Reale in Monza. Bresci was sentenced to life in prison. But in May 1901, he was found dead in his cell with a noose tied around his neck.

In the 1980s, a committee of socialists, communists, a Christian Democrat, Republicans, and anarchists in Carrara called for a monument to be built dedicated to Bresci as the avenger of the oppressed. Opponents railed against the monument in the Catholic newspaper Avvenire, making the argument that it "glorified murder," while supporters retorted, "It is not a monument to violence, but rather it is a monument against injustice and tyranny." In the end, the city government relented. The monument, a giant white marble block, today stands on the green space in front of the municipal cemetery.

Address Cimitero di Turigliano, Viale XX Septembre, at Via Aurelia, 54100 Massa |
Getting there From Florence take the A 12 toward Genova / Parma. Take the exit for
Massa Carrara, then continue toward the Marina Carrara. Take the main road Viale XX
Septembre to the roundabout at the intersection of SS 1 Aurelia (in the middle is a large
white obelisk). The park will be on the left. | **Tip** More rebels are buried nearby in graves
without crosses, including Giuseppe Pinelli, who was accused of orchestrating the
1969 attack on an agricultural bank on the Piazza Fontana, and came to his death by
"falling" from a fourth-story window while in police custody.

12 — The Mural of Francesca Rolla

Uprising on the Piazza delle Erbe

It was July 7, 1944. The partisans were hiding out in the mountains and the women of Carrara acted as a lifeline to them, delivering messages and food. The Italian peninsula was divided by the so-called Gothic Line – at the same latitude as Massa-Carrara and Pesaro – a fortified front established by German soldiers and prisoners of war after the landing of the Allied troops in Sicily in 1943 to halt the Allied advance into the Po Valley.

The National Socialists gave the command to evacuate Carrara in order to weaken the resistance groups in the surrounding area. Francesca Rolla, leader of the resistance, mobilized her comrades, "No, we will not leave the city!" Schools and businesses closed, but on the Piazza delle Erbe the women of the market threw the contents of their vegetable stalls on the ground. They stood just inches from the Nazi machine guns, armed only with anger and determination: "Our approach not only impressed the whole city, but also the Germans; they were actually afraid of us, we were like wild beasts to them."

Just four days later, the Germans recanted their order to evacuate the town. Carrara and the villages in the surrounding mountains had been freed by the anarchist partisans. Unlike the rest of northern Italy, in Carrara the anarchist movement remained strong. The marble workers preferred their own politics and forms of opposition over the communists' mass organization.

Francesca Rolla (1915 – 2010) remained president of the partisan organization (A.N.P.I.) in the province of Carrara until her death. In tribute to her service, six artists painted an enormous mural of Rolla in the Piazza delle Erbe. To this day, on the first of May, an anarchist demonstration is held there.

Address Piazza delle Erbe, 54033 Carrara | Getting there Piazza delle Erbe is located in the center of Carrara as the extension of Vicolo del Duomo, near the cathedral. | Tip Just a few streets away, in the Enoteca Velia at Via A. Manzoni 1, you can find delicacies from the mountains, and wines from around the world.

13 The Sculptures of Mario Del Sarto

An open-air museum on the road to Colonnata

Michelangelo himself visited Colonnata in order to choose the gleaming white marble he would use for his sculptures. On the road that leads up into the mountains, you can see, standing before the Museo del Cavatore (Museum of the Quarry Worker) a copy of the Ferrovia Marmifera, the locomotive from the 19th century used well into the 1960s that brought the marble blocks from the quarries out into the valley. A bit farther on stands a replica of the *David* in all its glory.

Past the village of Canalie and around a steep curve, majestic white figures dot the slopes along the road, all works by the sculptor Mario Del Sarto. Naturally, they are made of marble, but they do not necessarily comply with the classical ideal of beauty.

The sculptor is closely linked to Carrara and its marble. Until his retirement, he was an engineer on a *Marmifera* for 40 years, after which he began to work more creatively with marble. In doing so, he followed his instincts, or perhaps listened to the blocks of marble, which he claimed whispered their stories to him. In fact, just as with Michelangelo, his art seemed to take shape through the removal of the superfluous and the freeing of the figure trapped therein.

Sarto's *sculpture primitive* ("primitive sculptures"), as he calls his works, often tell stories of a religious nature. His sculpture of the manger relates that there is only one God; the statue of Pope Wojtyla was named *The Thought* and depicts the Pope as a young priest.

Del Sarto does not use material that was hewn from the mountains of marble, but rather pieces of stone that were left behind. There are many tales told in Del Sarto's open air museum. Meanwhile, at nearly 90 years of age, he is still in his studio every day and receives visitors.

Address Via Colonnata, 54033 Carrara | Getting there From the center of Carrara, take the Via Carriona eastward until you reach Via Colonnata. | Hours Daily 9am–6pm | Tip The best restaurant in Colonnata to try the region's famous lardo is the Locanda Apuana at Via Comunale 1 (www.locandaapuana.com).

14 Via Carriona
The ancient versus the zeitgeist

Via Carriona, which leads from the sea and the harbor up to the marble quarry in the mountains, was for many centuries the lifeblood of the city, though today it seems rather sleepy. In the old warehouses and buildings, however, many young artists have established their studios. Around 160 artist workshops are spread throughout the city. Many are graduates of the Accademia di Belle Arti in Carrara. The range of disciplines represented is broad: painters, sculptors, graphic designers, ceramic artists, photographers, and more.

The Villain, *The Jump*, *The Badly Behaved*, and *The Harlequin* – these are the names that Sabina Feroci has given her sculptures from the series *Figures of the Road*, which were mostly created using the artistic technique of paper on a metal structure. The artist has lived and worked in Carrara for many years. Her works contradict the laws of classical sculpture even in her choice of materials – and they are very successful. Feroci's studio is located at Via Carriona 3, but she has been exhibited around the world.

The Russian painter Anna Sirota works in the same space as Feroci, and just a few doors down is the workshop of sculptor Vanda Pianini, who has just recently undertaken a public contract for a community in Germany. Arianna Loscialpo creates bronze sculptures in her nearby studio, and twins Andrea and Simone Dell'Amico design objects in ceramic and marble.

At Il Cavallo, a trattoria and pizzeria located on Via Carriona across the street from the unfinished Roman sculpture of the same name, the artists gather on their lunch breaks or for happy hour, along with the professors of the Accademia and their students. The proprietor and his two daughters provide delicious home cooking at student-appropriate prices. In summertime, they serve fresh fish, otherwise often salt cod, and their specialty is the *taglierini* with broad beans.

Address Via Carriona 8–20, 50433 Carrara | **Getting there** From the cathedral, cross the Ponte alle Lacrime and turn right onto Via Carriona. | **Tip** The sculpture *Il Cavallo (The Horse)* across from the trattoria depicts the Roman soldier Marcus Curtius, who, according to legend, fought against slave labor in the quarries and before whom the *Carrarini* took off their hats when passing.

15 __ Padule di Fucecchio

Italy's largest wetland

To recount the history of the wetlands in Tuscany, one should start with those that are still remaining: nearly 4,450 acres south of the Apennines in the province of Pistoia between Montalbano and the hills of Cerbaie. Some 570 of those are protected in a nature reserve. Therefore, the Padule di Fucecchio is currently the largest marshland in Italy.

The wetlands were formed hundreds of years ago by the tributaries of the Arno River, whose sources lie in the Apennines and Montalbano. Today's wetlands make up an area that is only a tiny portion of their formerly massive extent, which once covered almost the entire region of the southern Valdinievole. The Etruscans began to cut intersecting canals into the area, a practice later perfected by the Romans, in order to make the land usable.

Even though the reserve is relatively small today, it still provides a safe habitat for many rare species of animals and plants. This particular microclimate hosts more than 150 bird species whose survival elsewhere is relatively uncommon: the family of Charadriidae (including plovers and turnstones), little grebes, gray herons, great bitterns, Eurasian wigeons, northern lapwings, water rails, moorhens, Eurasian coots, mallards, swallows, larks, sparrows, common teals, and many more. A highlight in the springtime is the impressive flight of the cranes. Moreover, some 800 pairs of black-crowned night herons and great white herons fly over the wetlands along with various species of Ibis.

The Research Center of the Wetlands organizes field trips through the unique reed and sedge landscape, with thematic and seasonal focuses. Visitors can see various plants, including the white and yellow water lilies that turn the surface of the marsh into a colorful tapestry. And if you choose a night tour, you can listen to "bird concerts" in the moor and enjoy a breathtaking sunset.

Address Via Castelmartini 115, 51036 Castelmartini, Larciano, www.zoneumidetoscane.it, fucecchio@zoneumidetoscane.it | Getting there Take the SS Firenze-Pisa-Livorno to the San Miniato exit and head toward Montecatini Terme. After Fucchecchio, take the SS 436, and after about seven miles you'll see the church of Castelmartini; the entrance to the nature reserve is located near the bar Le Morette. | Hours Mar–Oct, guided tours on the weekend | Tip You can learn about the development of the wetlands at the museum in Fucecchio at Piazza Vittorio Veneto 27 (www.comune.fucecchio.fi.it).

16___The Alimentari Forno Giotto
The best schiacciata

This shop is actually just a small grocery store located in a village hardly anyone has heard of. Yet a long line snakes its way out the front door and into the street during peak hours. Why? Because Italians want their *schiacciata*.

Florentines will often trek the six miles out into the hills of Scandacci – and spend considerable time waiting on line – to indulge in this regional snack. In terms of *schiacciata*, Giotto is an institution in and around Florence, and its Facebook page has more than 7,000 fans. The specialty bread – in reality just a simple flatbread made from wheat flour – is prepared here according to an ancient recipe, exactly as it has been since 1953.

The secret: years of experience and special ingredients: flour and olive oil. You will understand why it is worth all the effort as soon as you take your first bite, because the *schiacciata* (which in English means "pressed together") is always straight from the oven. Crispy on the outside, hot on the inside, it is produced for the masses as if on an assembly line.

The boss is the most involved of the staff, either cutting the fresh bread or rushing to the oven behind the counter to pull out the loaves at exactly the right moment. The most important thing is the baking time: 32 minutes – no more, no less. Others may bake it for only 20 minutes, but it won't have the same taste. You can top your bread with *mortadella* (the mild salami from Tuscany), *porchetta* (a refined and spiced pork), *lardo di colonnata* (the bacon from Carrara loved by gourmets), or some slices off the giant hams that hang on the wall.

On sunny days you can take your treat across the street, where you can sit at a table with a glass of wine and enjoy the scenery over the hills.

Address Via Volterrana 275, 50026 Chiesa Nuova | Getting there Chiesanuova is about 8.5 miles southwest of Florence. Through the Porta Romana, follow the Via Senese, which becomes the Strada Provinciale Volterrana, then turn left onto Via Volterrana. | Tip Nearby is the Agriturismo Massanera at Via Faltignano 68–76 (www.massanera.com), a comfortable lodging offering delicious farm products: olive oil, ham, and salami from Cinta Senese pigs, and strong Chianti wine.

17 __ The Romanesque Church
Worshipping in the time of the Romans

Today, this is one of the more tranquil and deserted corners of the Lunigiana region in the province of Massa-Carrara. The view is spectacular, the silence almost mystical. But that was not always the case. The name *Lunigiana* originally came from the city of Luni, a major trading center on the Mediterranean in pre-Roman times. Back then, this was a strategically important spot, located just a couple miles from the village of Codiponte with its bridge over the River Aulella, which represented an important link from the sea to the north, that is from Luni to Lucca.

For this reason, the most beautiful Romanesque church of Lunigiana was built in the 12th century on exactly this spot. It included a basilica with six pillars supporting archways and a wooden ceiling: all very simple, yet the Romanesque building exudes a sense of dignity.

On the inside, the church is characterized by lavish decorations in the side portals and capitals. They are decorated with ornamentation representing such themes as the tree of life and with different floral elements like the lily or six-petal daisy.

Even the church's name is suggestive of its meaning: *Capite Pontis*, Latin for "bridgehead," is located on a spur of the ancient Via Francigena – already a place of worship in pre-Roman times. A baptismal font was found buried underground here, proof that from the beginning, the church served as a baptistery for virtually the entire region of the Apuan Alps and the Apennines.

The most significant work of art in the church – which is dedicated to Saints Cornelio and Cipriano – is the triptych *Madonna con il Bambino*, and the building itself is also among the most important monuments of the Lunigiana. The bell tower, constructed in the 17th century, was restored in the 1970s and shines in all its original splendor.

Address Localitá Codiponte, 54014 Casola in Lunigiana | Getting there Codiponte
is located approximately 25 miles north of Carrara, either via the A 12 (exit Aulla, then
via the SS 62 toward Casola in Lunigiana to Loc. Codiponte) or on the (winding)
SS 446 toward Casola in Lunigiana to Codiponte. | Hours Always open | Tip Only
six miles away in the town of Equi Terme, a thermal spa offers a refreshing respite
(www.termediequi.it).

18__Casa Villa Carlo Pepi

The Don Quixote of art

Carlo Pepi has always trusted his intuition. It was what helped him expose the forgeries that were alleged to be by Michelangelo and Picasso. "A fake does not vibrate, it sounds dull, like a badly tuned bell."

Guided only by instinct, Carlo Pepi has accumulated 20,000 pieces of art by more than 2,000 artists. He has even bought pictures at flea markets, following the artists thereafter as they matured in their careers. In his collection also lies a treasure trove of documents from the lives of artists such as Amedeo Modigliani, as well as drawings by Francesco Gioli – and even sketches by Picasso.

Above all, his collection features works by *Macchiaioli*, a group of painters who were part of a movement against dogmatism in art from 1855 to 1865, characterized by spotted colored surfaces. Pepi has acquired over 700 works by the movement's most famous representative, Giovanni Fattori. Though the images were frowned upon by the majority of the art world, Carlo Pepi viewed them as innovative.

Every spare lira Pepi earned during his career – he is now 73 years old – was invested in art. After studying business administration, he advised companies as a freelancer, and when at times that did not bring in enough income to support his passion for collecting, he took out loans to buy new works.

For many years, Pepi has lived here in the charming village of Crespina, home to many artists decades ago. When Pepi leads visitors through the 30 rooms of his villa, he points out all the pictures that hang unassumingly on the walls, explaining the compositions of color and recounting details of the artists' lives, as he sprints from image to image. Sometimes you may have difficulty keeping up with him, but the art is completely accessible to those who visit, speaking a language that's understandable to all.

Address Villa Fattoria Montelisi, Piazza del Comune Villa-Museo at Via i Gioielli 13/15, 56040 Crespina, www.casamuseopepi.it, pepicarlo@libero.it | Getting there Crespina is located about 19 miles southeast of Pisa. Take the SGC Firenze-Pisa-Livorno to the Lavoria exit and continue toward Canaia, then turn left onto the SP 35 to Crespina. The villa is on the town square. | Hours Guided tours available by appointment, email pepicarlo@libero.it. For the collection of Macchiaioli painters in Livorno, email museofattori@comune.livorno.it. | Tip In the neighboring village of Fauglia you'll find a museum dedicated to the spot painter Kienerk.

19__ The Former Salt Storehouse

A red house with green bottles

Just over 12 miles west of Florence, between the Arno and Elsa rivers, lies the town of Empoli and its 40,000 residents. In the middle of the town's historic center, with its picturesque collegiate church of Sant'Andrea and the Fontana del Pampaloni, stands a bulky construction of red stone. The building, which dates from the 14th century, served for a long time as a storehouse for salt.

The salt originated in the salt mines of Volterra, some 30 miles away. At that time, it was transported on the backs of donkeys and came to Empoli by way of the former Via degli Asini, or "street of the donkeys," known today as Via Ridolfi. The salt was stored here and was then either distributed elsewhere or sold directly to customers – primarily to the peasant farm families of the area. The allocation per person per year was carefully regulated. The majority of the precious resource was transported from the warehouse by ships on the Arno down to Florence. In the 18th century, the building underwent a major expansion, and it can be admired to this day in this enlarged form.

Through legislative changes in the late 18th and 19th centuries, the salt storehouse lost its status as a central repository and was abandoned. The historic building only came back into favor when it was chosen to house the town's glass museum. Empoli became famous in more recent times for its glassmaking – the city supplied the surrounding areas with bottles to be used in the olive oil and wine industries. Originally known for its production of green glass, from the 1950s onward, the town also produced white and colored glass. A trip through the museum's remarkable and comprehensive collection gives visitors many interesting facts about the history of the glass industry.

Address Via Ridolfi 70, 50053 Empoli, www.museodelvetrodiempoli.it | **Getting there**
Empoli is located about 19 miles west of Florence on the SGC Firenze-Pisa-Livorno. Take
the Empoli Est exit. The Muve (Museo del Vetro) is located in the town center, northeast
of the collegiate church. | **Hours** Tue–Sun 10am–7pm | **Tip** The Pizzeria Santo Stefano
at Via Santo Stefano 8, open daily 6pm–midnight, serves pizza made with organic
ingredients, and fresh draft beer.

20__Fattoria di Maiano
The romantic park of the queen

British politician and well-traveled art connoisseur Sir John Temple-Leader (1810–1903) found true love in Cannes, where he met Maria Luisa de'Leoni from Lucca. Together, they ventured to Florence, where he bought land – but he didn't exactly purchase a lush, blooming landscape.

The location of Temple-Leader's estate in the hills between Fiesole and Settignano was enviable, but the buildings were in ruins, and the more than 1,700 acres looked like they belonged on the moon. For centuries, sedimentary rock had been mined in quarries here to build magnificent buildings elsewhere, and only stone skeletons remained.

Temple-Leader began an extensive reforestation, planting cypresses and pine trees, restored the *fattoria*, or farm, and repurposed the convent buildings into an agricultural village. Along both banks of the small Mensola River, he extended the "pillars" of the local quarry. These rock formations were so named because they were the source of the stone used to create the pillars of the Capella dei Medici in Florence. He also built a bizarre tower, with its balcony overlooking an idyllic lake, for his beloved wife, Maria Luisa. Additionally, he created an amusement park for visitors from all over the world, including a small changing cottage for guests who wished to swim, and tables for picnicking. Pathways once used by stonemasons were transformed into walking trails.

Even Queen Victoria came to the park's 1888 dedication ceremony, and the *Illustrated London News* printed a watercolor of the queen entranced by the romance of the place.

Today, three generations of the Conte Miari Fulcis family – the heirs of the estate – have brought Temple-Leader's ideas back to life, operating the estate's farm and bed & breakfast and maintaining the site. Residents of Florence travel up here on Sundays to spend a relaxing day in the countryside.

Address Via Cave di Maiano 2, 50014 Fiesole, www.fattoriadimaiano.com | Getting there From Florence, follow signs for Fiesole from the Piazza della Libertà and Viale Don Minzoni. On Viale Augusto Righi take the turn to Cave di Maiano, then follow the signs for Fattoria di Mainao. | Tip The Conte Miari Fulcis family manufactures an award-winning olive oil at the Fattoria di Maiano.

21 Naturalmente Lunigiana

Cheese and sausage from happy cows and pigs

The scenery is straight out of a storybook, the way you've always pictured it: there are goats in the mountains, cows grazing peacefully on the wide meadow, satisfied pigs wallowing in the mud, and chickens clucking excitedly in the yard.

On the farm of Pier Paolo Piagneri, the pastures stretch dreamily at an altitude of over 3,280 feet in the Apuan Alps. The farm itself is rather small, but the four donkeys, 27 head of cattle, 16 buffalos, 180 pigs, 100 rabbits, and 200 hens and roosters are truly treated with respect, and each lives and is cared for according to its species-specific needs.

Since 1996, when Pier Paolo turned his back on his career in the financial industry, he and his small crew have produced cheese and cured meats, all from their own animals. The products are all made according to the old recipes of the Lunigiana region.

There is, for example, the *Montelusci* – a mountain cheese produced in the summertime – made from a mix of cow's milk, sheep's milk, and goat's milk. The hard cheese, aged up to 18 months, tastes rather spicy, thanks to the herbs from the mountain grasslands. Then there is the *Stella dell'arpa* (which translates to "alpine star" in the dialect of the region), made from 70 percent cows' milk and 30 percent buffalos' milk. The *Mortadella della Lunigiana* is a soft salami made out of the best pieces of the pig, as it is not part of local tradition to smoke ham. And don't forget the *salsiccie*, or sausages. They are made from the meat of pigs known as the Grigio Toscano, a cross of the famous Cinta Senese that have been bred in Siena for over 1,000 years, and the Duroc, one of the old stock pig breeds from the United States. Only salt, pepper, and herbs are added to the sausage meat – they are a true delicacy.

Those who are interested may visit the animals and the farm and get to know the lucky residents.

Address Tenuta "La Giara," shop is Località Pala di Scorcetoli, Via Nazionale 42, 54023 Filattiera, naturalmentelunigiana@gmail.com | Getting there Coming from the A 15 (Parma-La Spezia) and E 33, take the exit for Pontremoli, then follow the signs for Filattiera. | Hours Make a reservation at least one week in advance by email | Tip In the shop Naturalmente Lunigiana in Pontremoli at Via Ricci Armani 2, besides the sausages and cheeses, you can purchase jams, honey, and the local pasta specialty, *testaroli*

22_Antica Farmacia Münstermann

Pioneer of homeopathy

When Francesco Münstermann opened his homeopathic pharmacy in Florence, it was the first in all of Tuscany that offered alternative medicines and remedies. His original best seller was an ointment made from a pure plant base with arnica – known for centuries as a natural remedy for pain. His calendula cream was also frequently in high demand for itch relief.

Münstermann had such great success not only with his new medicines, but also with other plant-based products, that, in 1908, he was able to move his business into a stately new storefront located on Piazza Goldoni. He called his pharmacy the Farmacia Anglo-Americana, in the hopes of attracting clientele from the large community of Anglo-Americans who lived in Florence at the time. He kept the name until 1935, when he changed it to Farmacia Münstermann because of racial laws imposed in Italy by the fascist regime.

Although the building suffered extensive damage during the great flood of 1966, the original interior has almost been completely preserved. Münstermann also did well with his own cosmetics back then, individually tailored to suit each customer. He wrote down all of his recipes in a book that his heirs consult to this day in order to manufacture their products.

Visitors who enter the Farmacia Münstermann are often enraptured by the wood-paneled interior, and are equally taken by the fact that Dottoressa Petruzzi is still selling the same products that have been available here since the 18th century. The eau de toilette, now the shop's most sought-after creation, and the honey-almond cream, are both made meticulously following the original recipes of Münstermann.

Address Piazza Carlo Goldoni 2r, 50123 Florence | **Getting there** Bus 6 to the Vigna Nova stop | **Hours** Tue–Sat 10am–1pm and 2–7pm | **Tip** There is a lovely small hotel with 20 rooms called the Hotel Goldoni nearby, at Borgo Ognissanti 8 (www.hotelgoldoni.com).

23 The Arno and its Valley

A naked couple at the station

Upon arriving at the main train station in Florence, the majority of people make a beeline straight across the square in the direction of the city center. However, if instead you follow the sidewalk to the left along the station building, you will discover a nude couple in marble sitting before an austere white building on the corner. The name of this sculpture from 1935 is *L'Arno e la Sua Valle* (*The Arno and its Valley*), a work by Italo Griselli (1880–1958). A man and a woman are seated next to each other, relaxed and dignified. Arno, the male figure, supports his arm casually on an oversized snail. The female figure caresses a little lamb.

Griselli was well regarded by his fellow artists and critics, and up until 1914 had worked in many different cities around the world, including St. Petersburg, Berlin, and Paris. Returning to Italy, he created, among other things, the "fascist salute" in marble for Mussolini's regime in Rome.

He received the contract for the decorative work of art in Florence from his friend, the famous architect Giovanni Michelucci, who belonged to the group of architects called the Gruppo Toscano. The decor for the entire train station, including the Palazzina Reale, was designed by Michelucci and is a prime example of rational architecture. Michelucci wanted to enrich this "royal palace," which was planned for the reception of government leaders, with the decorative marble sculpture outside.

Griselli first gave the allegorical pair their foundation atop a stone square. He then worked on the two figures for many months. From the original rather idealized models, the marble man and woman gradually developed their own individual personalities. And at their inauguration in 1935, both the train station and *The Arno and its Valley* were celebrated as outstanding works of art and architecture.

Address Piazza Adua, Florence 50123 | **Getting there** Bus 6, 11, 12, to the Santa Maria Novella Train Station stop | **Tip** In the station at platform 8, a plaque memorializes the more than one thousand Jews who were deported to concentration camps from here.

24__Bar Marisa
Alé Viola!

For those just looking to grab a coffee, it appears to be a normal bar. But for fans of the Fiorentina soccer club, the Bar Marisa is a holy temple. "A hunchback should never set foot in here," it is said. And by "hunchback" they mean fans of Juventus Turin, the arch-enemy of *La Viola* ("The Violets"), as the Florentine players are referred to thanks to the color of their jerseys. The *Gobbi* ("Hunchbacks") are so-called because Juventus is always suspected of making their backs "crooked" in order to gain favorable referee rulings on the field. Though others claim the nickname harkens back to the '50s, when the design of the uniforms caused the backs of the players' shirts to puff up with air when they ran.

The unity between *città* and *squadra* – that is, between a city and its soccer team – is strong throughout Italy, but nowhere more so than in Florence. After winning the championship in 1956 and 1969, the flag of the Fiorentina flew atop the Palazzo Vecchio, and the team's victories were celebrated with Vespa parades up to Piazzale Michelangelo. The soul of *La Viola* lives in the Bar Marisa, and soccer is the only acceptable topic of conversation here. Pictures of the team's biggest stars hang on the walls, of course. This is also the seat of the *università del calcio*, the university of soccer, full of discussions and opinions about current games and players.

This meccalike meeting place for fans is directly opposite Artemio Franchi stadium. Some patrons in the bar will object to a call by a referee against their team with a *caffè della protesta* ("protest coffee") after hearing the loud jeers coming from the Curva Fiesole – the area at the northern end of the stadium where the most enthusiastic and vocal spectators sit. Sitting here before or after a game, you may also catch a glimpse of a star player coming or going from the offices of AC Fiorentina across the way, and the entrance to the VIP stands is right on the corner. You can't get more "midfield" than that.

Address Viale Manfredo Fanti 41, 50137 Florence | **Getting there** Bus 3, 11, 17, to the San Gervasio stop | **Tip** Explore soccer history at the soccer museum, the Museo del Calcio, at Viale Aldo Palazzeschi 20 (www.museodelcalcio.it).

25 Boutique della Pasta Fresca

Just like Grandma makes

The production of handmade pasta was originally the main business of this small shop, which is situated on a side street in a residential neighborhood near the Piazza delle Cure, between the lively Piazza della Libertà and the soccer stadium.

The business is run by three young people: Fabrizio, who grew up in the mountainous region about 25 miles from Florence; Francesco, who has Neapolitan roots; and Patrizia, a Florentine. They began to sell handmade pasta here in 1997. The store's first patrons were housewives shopping for freshly made tortellini, ravioli, and tagliatelle. Over time, the first four tables were set up and you could find a plate of warm pasta at lunchtime. Eventually, workers and laborers from throughout the neighborhood started coming for lunch. The food was so well received that a line now forms at peak hours.

On the menu, you'll find simple dishes, often based on rural cuisine – the type of food you might be served at an Italian grandma's house. The pasta is sometimes made partly from chestnut flour, the tradition in Mugello, where Fabrizio's father is from. A sauce with tripe, *alla trippa*, a classic here in Florence, is often available. Or there might be pasta with mushrooms, pesto, or *polpettine* (small meatballs in tomato sauce), which is extremely popular in the south of Italy.

The restaurant is tiny, with only six tables. The lines are long and the turnover is quick, so at midday things move swiftly. Nobody has ever complained. A plate of pasta and a glass of wine guarantee a good mood for all. Most important, the atmosphere here is informal, and the prices reasonable. And just like at Grandma's, they also serve desserts, including delicious crepes with Nutella and whipped cream.

Address Via Domenico Cirillo 2c, 50133 Florence | Getting there Bus 1, 21, to the Pontealle Riffe stop | Hours Daily 8am–2:30pm, 4–7pm, closed Wed and Sat evenings | Tip Located nearby on Via Faentina, the small, inviting park Area Pettini-Burresi is perfect for a break.

26 The Brancacci Chapel's Secret

Masaccio's hidden self-portrait

The fresco cycle in the Brancacci Chapel is an impressive work of art; it comprises individual works that were painted over time on three walls of the chapel by a trio of great Renaissance artists. Felice Brancacci, a silk merchant and the ambassador to Egypt, had initially engaged the artist Masolino. Then the young Masaccio was asked to continue the work, and finally Filippino Lippi. It took 60 years for all the frescoes to be finished.

Upon entering the chapel, the magnificence of this ensemble is almost overwhelming. But in the twelve biblical scenes, there is one representation that is of particular interest. On the lower picture field of the left wall is *The Throne of Saint Peter – The Resurrection of the Son of Theophilus*. It depicts how Peter raised the dead son of the governor of Antioch and how – as a reward – a church with a *cathedra* (a bishop's chair) was built in his honor.

On the right side, you can see a group of three apostles. The young man who is looking out of the picture is a self-portrait of Masaccio, "in which he is depicted so superbly that he seems to be alive."

Masaccio was close friends with Brunelleschi – the Grand Master who oversaw construction of the cathedral's dome – and on the right edge of the picture stands Filippo Brunelleschi, wearing a black hood. This is his only contemporary portrait.

Sadly, the young artist left this work unfinished; he died on a trip to Rome at the age of 26 under mysterious circumstances. Some believe an envious competitor had a hand in his death. Florentine crime writer Nino Filastò speculated about the details surrounding Masaccio's demise in his suspenseful novel *Aringa Rossa*. Secret societies and conspiracies play a role.

Address Piazza del Carmine, Florence 50124 | Getting there Bus D to the Carmine stop | Hours Weekdays 10am–5pm, holidays from 1pm | Tip The simple Trattoria Angiolino, at Via di Santo Spirito 36 (12:30–2:30pm and 7:30–11:30pm), serves original Tuscan cuisine.

27 __ Buchette del Vino
Street vending in the 16th century

In some palazzi you will notice strange arched windows on the ground floor. Occasionally, the arch is closed with a small wooden door; sometimes it is even bricked over. On Via delle Belle Donne, near such an opening, you can still read some writing on the wall: "Open from November to April from nine o'clock in the morning to two o'clock in the afternoon and from five o'clock to eight o'clock in the evening," along with the word *cantina*, or "cellar." In the city, there are 20 or so of these covered-over windows. But what exactly is, or was, sold there?

Well, these were the very first kiosks in the city, called *buchette* (literally, "small holes"), which peddled wine from the nearby vineyards.

At the end of the 15th century, the heyday of cloth production in Florence was coming to a close. Manufacturers from northern Europe and England became the market leaders and controlled the economic events in medieval Europe from then on.

The financial sector, which had enriched the city of Florence to this point, began to falter, and the great Florentine families lost their fortunes. Many had to find new sources of income and began to think about investing in their land: they began cultivating grapes and olives. To bypass the middlemen and maximize profits, these new winemakers sold their product directly from ground-floor windows over the cellars where the barrels were housed.

Sales flourished, the clientele was broadly based, and the atmosphere was always optimal. To protect themselves from drink-happy thieves, the opening was only big enough for a *fiasco* (then the standard wine bottle in Tuscany, see p. 208) to pass through. Customers came with empty bottles and left with them full. Many of the medieval kiosks are now gone, but a precious few have been transformed into colorful mailboxes or other decorative elements.

Address Via delle Belle Donne 2, 50123 Florence | Getting there Bus 6, 11, 12, 36, to the Santa Maria Novella Station stop | Tip Further examples of buchette can be admired in the Palazzo Strozzi, Piazza degli Strozzi, and at the Arco di San Pierino in Santa Croce, as well as in San Niccolò.

28 Canto dei Bischeri

A greedy reminder

It was a matter of prestige when the construction of the Duomo began in 1295: a status symbol for the city's newly won self-confidence, power, and wealth. The official name of the cathedral, Santa Maria del Fiore, or Our Lady of the Flower, refers to Florence's coat of arms with its lily.

After the initial planning stages, it became clear that quite a number of buildings would have to be demolished in order to make room for the major project, which would stand on a total area of nearly 90,000 square feet.

At the corner of what is now the Via dell'Oriuolo, you can read a sign with the inscription *Canto dei Bischeri*. The Bischeri were a Florentine family who owned a handful of houses on this spot when the construction of the Duomo began. Like all other homeowners in the area, they were offered a "fair price" for their property so that they would vacate the premises. But the Bischeri refused. A second, more generous offer was also unsuccessful in persuading the family to move.

The family was obviously using time to their advantage: the further the construction progressed, the larger the problem became, and the more bargaining power the Bischeri had. They even rejected a third, astronomically high, bid. And then, the following night, the houses of the Bischeri were set ablaze. This incident resulted in the financial and social decline of the family. They had to leave the area without receiving a dime; at that time, insurance did not exist. Their descendants once again made their fortunes in Florence some two hundred years later, but this time with the name Guardagni, for the shame of their former surname was still too great.

Since then, *Bischeri* has come to mean "dummy" to the Florentines. In fact, you'll often hear someone on the street call out, *"O bischero!"* But it's usually meant in jest.

VIA DELL'ORIUOLO

GIA
VIA DEGLI ALBERTINELLI

CANTO
DEI
BISCHERI

Address Piazza del Duomo/corner of Via dell'Oriuolo, 50122 Florence | Getting there Bus C2 to the Tosinghi stop | Tip You can trace the construction of the cathedral at the museum of the Duomo (www.operaduomo.firenze.it).

29 _ Chiostro dello Scalzo

The stillness of the frescoes

Andrea del Sarto was one of the true artistic geniuses of the Renaissance. His painting of *The Last Supper* in the church of San Salvi is surely one of the highlights of his career, and several of his other works are exhibited in the Uffizi Galleries. There is, however, an opportunity to enjoy a masterpiece by this great artist in perfect peace and quiet. The entrance that leads to this unique fresco cycle, not far from the bustling Piazza San Marco, is open just a few days a week for a limited number of hours. Today this former cloister with six columns in the Renaissance style is fully covered, and all of its walls are decorated with frescoes that tell stories from the life of John the Baptist, painted by Del Sarto.

Del Sarto received this commission from a religious order referred to as *dello scalzo*, or "the barefoot" – so-called because the bearers of the cross walked barefoot in the confraternity's processions. The artist himself belonged to the brotherhood, officially named the *Compagnia dei Disciplinati di San Giovanni Battista* (Company of the Disciples of St. John the Baptist), which was founded in 1376. Like other religious orders, its membership consisted largely of laymen, but it was still recognized by the church. Their mission was to spread the faith. The individual fraternities were assigned specific activities: praying, teaching, or charity.

The brothers of the confraternity all wore black robes and hoods that covered most of their faces. Two of them can be seen flanking John the Baptist on the crescent-shaped relief above the entrance to the cloister.

The *chiaroscuro* technique used by Andrea del Sarto when he painted the 16 monochromatic frescoes between 1514 and 1526, when combined with the stillness of the place and the vivid representation, generate a strong meditative atmosphere in which you can truly enjoy this unique artwork.

Address Via Cavour 69, 50129 Florence | **Getting there** Bus, inter alia, 6, 7, 10, 14 to the Piazza San Marco stop | **Hours** Mon, Thurs and the 1st, 3rd, and 5th Sat of the month and 2nd and 4th Sun of the month 8:15am–1:50pm | **Tip** In the refectory of the convent of San Marco at Piazza San Marco 1, you can see a painting of *The Last Supper* by Domenico Ghirlandaio.

30 Church of San Leonardo in Arcetri

Dante's pulpit

Sunday is the perfect day for a stroll in the city. And the church of San Leonardo, one of the oldest houses of worship in Florence, can be reached via a romantic footpath outside the city gates. The walk to the church is full of atmosphere, and the narrow Via San Leonardo is lined with sloping chunky stone walls, behind which the villas of wealthy Florentines are hidden.

You'll pass the house where Tchaikovsky lived, and eventually arrive at Arcetri, where Galileo Galilei passed the final days of his life. The Romanesque church of San Leonardo in Arcetri appears a little way up on the left. Only the crescent above the entryway gleams in gold; the rest of the church is quite simple.

At 10:30 on Sunday mornings, thirty minutes before the holy mass at 11, Don Leonardo opens the doors of the church and lets both art lovers and the curious come in to admire a special work of art from the 12th century: the pulpit of white Carrara marble inlaid with dark green marble from Prato. This treasure stands inside on the left-hand side, and is decorated with marquetry work depicting scenes from the life of Jesus. The details merit a much closer look.

It is popularly referred to as "Dante's pulpit" because it's widely believed that the author of *The Divine Comedy* spoke from it in the church of San Pier Scheraggio, where political gatherings were held prior to the designation of the Palazzo della Signoria as the seat of government of Florence. Anyone who had something to say gave a speech from this spot.

The pulpit was restored to its original splendor in 2010 by the famous workshop Opificio delle Pietre Dure, which dates back to the time of the Medici.. Viewing it in the solitude and silence of this small church is a special pleasure.

Address Via San Leonardo di Arcetri 25, 50125 Florence | Getting there Bus 12, 13, 02 to the Galilei stop | Tip A nice walk to the church can be taken from the Ponte Vecchio along the Costa San Giorgio, where Galileo Galilei once lived in number 19, to Forte Belvedere, which continues as the Via San Leonardo beyond the city gates.

31 Confraternita della Misericordia

Men in black

Today, modern ambulances are parked in front of the dispatch center of the Venerabile Arciconfraternita della Misericordia di Firenze next to the cathedral. When an emergency call comes in, help is delivered by those wearing EU-standardized uniforms. But up until the year 2000, the volunteers at this private aid organization – the oldest in the world – were dressed in black robes with hoods covering their faces. Their irrefutable motto was: "absolute anonymity and completely free of charge."

The Confraternita della Misericordia (Confraternity of Mercy) in Florence, now in operation for nearly 800 years, was the first of its kind when it was called to life through the works of San Pietro of Verona (see p. 98) in 1244. Citizens of all walks of life – it's possible that Michelangelo was among them – banded together to "honor God through compassionate works of charity" and to spread the faith. Volunteers were required to wear the *buffa*, or hood, pulled over their faces, because it was only considered a good work before the Lord when it was selfless and anonymous.

The brothers helped the poorest of the poor, and they provided services that city leaders were unable or unwilling to offer. They took the sick and injured to the hospital, gave food to the destitute, and removed dead bodies from the streets. The city benefited from their assistance, especially during times of plague in the Middle Ages, when cleanliness meant survival.

The brothers also made their contributions to humanitarian disasters during the cholera epidemic, the two World Wars, and up until the great flood of 1966. The small museum tells the history of the confraternity over the centuries, and also has a small art collection with masterpieces by Luca della Robbia and Lorenz Ghiberti.

Address Piazza del Duomo 19/20, 50122 Florence | **Getting there** Bus C2 to the Tosinghi stop | **Hours** Museum: Mon 9am–12pm, Fri 4–5pm, and by request, email enrysantiny@hotmail.it | **Tip** The Grom ice-cream parlor at Via del Campanile 2, on the corner of Via delle Oche, serves delicious gelato, sorbet, and granita made from natural ingredients.

32 __ The Face of Michelangelo

The eternal lamenter

You have to look very, very closely, but once you find it, you'll be surprised by the precision that went into the drawing of this human head. It's in the Piazza della Signoria, just to the right of the entrance door to the Palazzo Vecchio, in the lower part of the wall: the profile of a man carved into the building's light brown stone.

The portrait is said to have been created by none other than the master Michelangelo himself. A copy of his *David*, perhaps the most famous and visited sculpture in the history of art, resides right next door to the palazzo, while the original stands nearby in the Galleria dell'Accademia.

According to legend, every time Michelangelo passed along the Via della Ninna, which runs right by the Palazzo Vecchio, he was harassed at night by a destitute man, who always told him the same old story: he was never repaid by any of the people to whom he loaned money, including Michelangelo. One night, when Michelangelo could not free himself from the clutches of the eternal lamenter, he disinterestedly reached for his tools and began to etch the profile of the man into the soft stone of the palazzo. He did so behind his back so that the man – who was confronting him face-to-face – would not notice that his portrait was being carved.

Another version of the legend claims that Michelangelo made the portrait of a man who was condemned to wear an iron collar as punishment for the non-payment of debts. The sentence was carried out in the Loggia dei Lanzi, next to the Palazzo Vecchio, and Michelangelo asked how long the culprit would be exhibited there in his horrible position for all to see. In response, one of the soldiers proclaimed to the master, "Not long enough," and thus he created the portrait on the spot as a memorial to the man.

Address Piazza della Signoria, Florence 50122 | Getting there Bus C 2 to the Condotta stop | Tip Delicious homemade chocolate is served at the Café Rivoire (www.rivoire.it).

33__Folon's Suitcase
A love letter to Florence

Jean-Michel Folon was just 20 years old in the 1950s when he visited Tuscany for the first time, hitchhiking with only a backpack. But he formed an intimate bond with Florence that endures well beyond his death.

Folon referred to his sculptures in the Rose Garden, which his widow bequeathed to the city of Florence, as simply "little men." They always seem to pop up unexpectedly in one corner of the park or another. One is under the constant subjection of an umbrella fountain, another is sitting on a bench. Folon even packed Florence into a suitcase, in the truest sense of the word. *Partir*, or "leaving," is the name of the sculpture located at the entrance to the Rose Garden just below the Piazzale Michelangelo. It is the frame of a large, rusty-looking suitcase with a boat cruising along inside. You can gaze through it at the wonders of the city: Palazzo Vecchio, Brunelleschi's dome, the cathedral of Santa Maria del Fiore – it is like a love letter to Florence.

By the 1960s, Folon had made a name for himself through his paintings and illustrations, including those made for Franz Kafka's works and for the *New Yorker*. His works have been exhibited in museums around the world, and his most famous piece, 1974's *The Death of a Tree*, is now in the Canton of Lugano's art museum.

In the Tuscan town of Pietrasanta, Folon began to work with sculptures, and Tuscany is where he left his heart: "My dream is to one day find a place in Tuscany with a garden and a beautiful house, where I can leave all my works." His wife, Paola Ghiringhelli Folon, fulfilled his wish, with the donation of twelve works, ten in bronze and two in plaster, to the city of Florence.

The park features more than 1,000 varieties of roses, and the unique atmosphere and fragrance allow you to enjoy the views from its terraces in a very special way.

Address The Rose Garden, Viale Giuseppe Poggi 2, 50125 Florence | Getting there Bus 13 to the Il David stop | Hours Daily 9am until sunset | Tip On the way back through the neighborhood of San Niccolò, drop in to the Enoteca Fuori Porta at Monte alle Croci 10r (www.fuoriporta.it) for lunch and a glass of wine.

34 __ The Fortepiano Workshop
The piano doctors

There are innumerable talented craftsmen and artisans in Florence who make shoes, weave silk, and design jewelry and furniture. But the work of Donatella Degiampietro, Antonella Conti, and Barbara Mingazzini is something very special. Their projects on historic pianos are a combination of detective work and precision restoration. There are no more than ten others in all of Italy who still specialize in their craft.

"When a piano comes in, we must decide which parts to leave and which parts to replace. The most difficult element is procuring spare parts. We will only strike it lucky at a select number of companies in the whole world. Some materials are particularly hard to find. There are English fortepianos, where whalebones are installed in the sound mechanism. We have even searched for old corsets and costumes that would sometimes contain whalebone. So we've combed through theatrical wardrobes here and there," explains Donatella, who has studied and worked in the United States at the Smithsonian Institution in Washington, D.C., and at the Metropolitan Museum of Art in New York City.

Here in San Frediano, Bartolomeo Cristofori invented the fortepiano in the 17th century. Haydn, Mozart, Beethoven, Schubert, and Schumann all played it. Between 1830 and 1850, it was replaced by the modern piano.

The academy right next door to the restoration workshop is named for the fortepiano's inventor. There are fourteen historic pianos on display and regular concerts are also held here (information can be found at www.accademiacristofori.it). The events in the small, intimate space are always elite – musicians come from all over the world, and can pick which of the unique instruments they wish to play. Alexander Lonquich, Jin Ju, and Malcolm Bilson have been honored guests.

Address Via di Camaldoli 9, 50124 Florence, ring the bell for the Laboratorio di Restauro, www.labfortepiano.it | **Getting there** Bus D from the train station to the Carmine stop | **Tip** The enchanting garden of the Torrigiani family at Via dei Serragli 144 (www.giardinotorrigiani.it) is the largest private garden in the city. Viewings are by appointment only (email info@giardinotorrigiani.it).

35 — Fountain House of the Villa Bandini

Cabinet of curiosities

On a side street off the well-trafficked Viale Europa is a hidden jewel from the summer culture of a time long past. Surrounded by a beautiful garden, here stands the 18th-century villa of the Bandini family, which later passed into the hands of the Marchesi Niccolini. Back then, in the unbearably hot summer months, the nobles would retire to their homes outside the city, where the climate was significantly cooler.

A kind of cabinet of curiosities was created in the garden's fountain house, or nymphaeum, by the Florentine sculptor Giuseppe Giovannozzi in 1746. In the middle is a large basin, which was at one time graced by a statue of Venus. On various sections of the walls, animal figures – monkeys, birds, and eagles – playfully push and shove mythological figures such as a dragon or a dwarf dressed as a nobleman. All the figures are made out of shells, coral, crystals, painted terra-cotta, and white and red marble.

The ceiling, decorated with a trompe l'oeil of a huge blue sky surrounded by trees and flying birds, catapults the viewer even deeper into the curious theatrical world. Artificial elements collide with nature, illustrating the struggle between art and nature in antiquity. This type of structure, with its artificially created grotto that harks back to ancient times, was being built in Italy as far back as 1500, but the nymphaeum here at the Villa Bandini was designed much later.

The artful garden, for the most part, no longer exists, but the villa itself now houses the city library for Quartiere 3. There you can obtain the key to see the curious works. The land on which the fountain house sits is now privately owned, but it was beautifully restored in 2000 and opened to the public.

Address Via del Paradiso 5, 50126 Florence | Getting there Bus 8, 31, 82, to the
Il Bandino, Euronics stop | Hours Key can be picked up in the library of the Quartiere 3,
Mon 2–7pm, Tue–Fri 9am–7pm, Sat 9am–1pm | Tip At Convivum, located at Viale
Europa 4/6 right on the corner, one can dine on delicious traditionally prepared Tuscan
specialties (www.conviviumfirenze.it).

36 __ Garden of the Vivarelli Colonna

Picnicking with Orpheus

The oversized wall in the middle of the artisans' quarter of Santa Croce stands out in a neighborhood where most houses are rather simple. But it's said that in the past, exuberant festivals were celebrated here. Driven by curiosity, neighbors would catch glimpses over the wall to see how the aristocracy amused themselves.

Approaching the park today through the entrance at Via delle Conce 28, you'll step into a dream world straight out of the 16th century. This small Italian garden was created in the 1610s by Francesco Maria Niccolò Gaburri. There are many fragrant lemon trees and in the center is a lovely swan fountain. Allow your gaze to sweep to the right, and you will come face-to-face with a statue of Orpheus – the singer and poet from Greek mythology – plucking his harp, surrounded by ornaments, and decorated with stalactites. The work has a somewhat melancholic effect, but it stands up admirably even in comparison to the world-famous grotto by Buontalenti in the Boboli Gardens.

Above Orpheus is the coat of arms of the Vivarelli Colonna family, who owned the property from 1857 until 1979, when the city of Florence took possession. Today, several of the city's ministries are housed in the grand structure, including those for culture and tourism.

Due to the financial difficulties of the municipality, the palazzo is currently up for auction. In the last round of bidding, the 43,000-square-foot property unfortunately did not find a new owner. The building is protected by historic preservation laws – thus, the commercial potential for the property remains limited. But that is a lucky thing for those who want to spend an afternoon in the little idyll with a view of Orpheus in the grotto.

Address Via Ghibellina 30, corner of Via delle Conce 28, 50122 Florence | Getting there
Bus C 2, C 3, to the Malborghetto stop | Hours Apr–Sep, Tue and Thu 10am–6pm | Tip
Until 1pm you can pick up delicious provisions for a picnic around the corner at the
Mercato Sant Ambrogio.

37 __ Giambologna's Devil
A misleading myth

On the corner of the Palazzo dei Vecchietti, a small devil sits about three stories up. You have to look very closely, but once you discover the bronze figure, you'll be impressed by its expressiveness. It was created by the Flemish artist Jean de Boulogne (1529–1608), better known as Giambologna, one of the leading sculptors of his time and the main representative of Mannerism, a period in European art that bridged the Renaissance and the Baroque. He created the *Rape of the Sabine Women* for the Loggia dei Lanzi in the Piazza della Signoria and the marble sculpture of the god Neptune in the fountain.

Giambologna's sponsor was Bernardo Vecchietti, a well-known patron of the arts. As the artist was passing through Florence on his travels, it was Vecchietti who persuaded him to stay for a while. In 1578, he commissioned Giambologna to decorate the new palace of his influential family with a devil figure. The artist then created a bracket to support a flagpole in the shape of a small devil.

Legend has it that Vecchietti sought to depict a story dating back to the year 1245, when the devil was defeated. An illustration of this same legend can also be seen in a fresco on the facade of the Loggia del Bigallo, across from the Baptistery (see p. 98). But in reality, it is not a devil but a satyr, a mythological figure that is half man and half goat.

As a thank-you, Giambologna gave his patron Bernardo yet another devil statue. It was attached to the palace across the road, which was also owned by the Vecchietti family. In their ignorance of the pagan background of the figures, the Florentine people called the intersection the *Canto dei diavoli*, or Corner of the Devils, which you can still read today on a street sign. The original sits in the Bardini museum. However, many consider the replica as impressive as the one in the museum.

Address Corner of Via dei Vecchietti / Via degli Strozzi, 50123 Florence | Getting there Bus C 2 to the Repubblica stop | Tip A few yards away in Piazza della Repubblica, you can enjoy delicious pastries and cappuccino in the historic Bar Paszkowski.

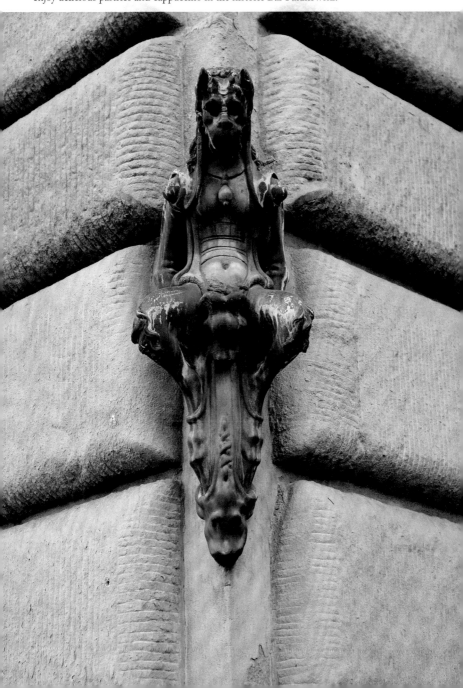

38__Good Friday in San Miniato

Hallelujah!

About 50 people silently follow the white-robed monks walking in prayer with their hoods drawn low over their faces. Don Bernardo carries the cross, leading the group as they rise up the stairs. In the darkness, only candles flicker on the way up to the last station of the Via Crucis: at the top, in front of the church of San Miniato, fantastic views of the city lights open up before you.

Whether you find yourself up here – so close to heaven – out of devotion to your belief in the Resurrection or simply to be enchanted by the lights of the city, this ceremony will immerse you in spirituality. Since 2012, every year on Good Friday, beginning at 9pm at the Piazzale della Basilica, the *Via Crucis* ritual is celebrated. And every year the 11 stations of the procession all follow a specific theme. Once it was "city," another year it was "fear," and yet another it was "life."

Accordingly, sometimes the Procession of the Cross passes through the nearby grove of cypress trees, other times through the cemetery where the tomb of the martyr San Miniato is located. Each place has its own mysterious mood. But the parade always ends with a view of the nighttime lights of Florence.

San Miniato al Monte is considered one of the most beautiful churches in Italy. The facade of the Romanesque church is clad in white Carrara marble and dark green serpentine from Prato. Its interior is a historical gem: the paved floor dates from 1207, the Capella del Crocefisso was created in 1448 by Michelozzo, and the terra-cotta decoration of the vault was done by Luca della Robbia.

At 7:15am and 5:30pm the small monastic community celebrates a mass featuring Gregorian chants, a mystical experience in itself, during which you can enjoy this lovely place without a stampede.

Address Via delle Porte Sante 34, 50125 Firenze, www.sanminiatoalmonte.it | **Getting there** Bus 12 from the train station to the San Miniato al Monte stop | **Hours** Daily 7am–7pm, in summer until sundown; closed weekdays from 1–4:30pm; from 7–8am only accessible by the Via delle Porte Sante entrance | **Tip** The monastery store sells ice cream, cookies, and homemade pastries.

39__The Head of Perseus

A statue's alter ego

It is one of the masterpieces on the Piazza della Signoria. The statue of Perseus stands in the Loggia dei Lanzi, a prime example of Florentine Gothic style. The bronze was created by the sculptor Benvenuto Cellini (1500–1571). The work, commissioned by Cosimo I, was meant to be a demonstration of the power of the Medici for the Florentine citizens who had freed Cosimo I from his enemies, the Republicans.

Thus stands the young, muscular Perseus wearing only a sash and a decorated winged helmet, triumphantly holding Medusa's head in one hand and in the other the sword with which he beheaded her. You can read about all this and more in any art guide. What is more interesting is that the artist has also created a portrait on the back of Perseus's head.

You have to enter the loggia and view the statue from behind to see that where the helmet meets the hair of the demigod, there is the face of a bearded old man. It is not the easiest to discover, because this spot is almost always in the shade, and it is difficult to detect the details of the roughly nine-foot-tall statue when it is backlit by the sun.

Cellini described the nine-year evolution of the Perseus statue (1545–1554) in his autobiography. With the "old man mask," he represented "a deliberate counterpoint to the youthful face of Perseus." This representation of dual faces was considered a symbol of wisdom, maintaining sight of both the past and future simultaneously, and this was probably meant to describe not just Perseus, but also Cosimo I.

However, many art connoisseurs are of the opinion that this is actually a self-portrait of the artist. Cellini's craving for recognition speaks to this notion. In his autobiography, he describes his artistic triumphs, but also exudes arrogance and selfishness.

Address Piazza della Signoria, 50122 Florence | **Getting there** Bus C 2 to the Condotta stop | **Tip** Atop the roof of the Loggia dei Lanzi is the bar of the Uffizi. In summer, the museums are open once a week until 10pm. An aperitif overlooking the square is lovely, thanks both to the view and the atmosphere (www.polomuseale.firenze.it).

40__ The High-water Marks

Reminders of the floods

On October 25, 1966, it started raining in Florence, and it seemed it would never stop. Violent downpours drenched the city, and the drainage system failed. The Arno overflowed its banks and inundated the streets, and on November 4, the bridgehead of the Ponte Vecchio was breached. *L'alluvione* ("the flood") was a historic moment in Florence, a fateful day for everyone who lived in the city at that time.

The flood swept half a million tons of sludge from the farmland of the Arno Valley into the city's historic center: approximately 10,000 shops, 8,000 workshops, and 600 industrial facilities were completely destroyed, and 21,000 homes were damaged. Even the Uffizi Galleries sustained damages: 60,000 books, 1,300 paintings, and works by Botticelli, Cimabue, and Donatello were ruined. The cost of a bottle of mineral water rose to ten times the normal price, and the government declared a state of emergency.

On the one hand, the world stood still. On the other, many Florentines don't remember 1966 as merely a year of disaster. The camaraderie of the young people who banded together to form volunteer aid troops is legendary to this day. Galeazzo Auzzi called his bronze sculpture *Angeli del Fango*, or Angels of the Mud, in honor of all the youths who rushed in to help in the aftermath of the flood.

Throughout the city, you can see the high-water marks that remain as reminders of the disaster. Many indicate not only the height of the water level of 1966, but also the flood of 1333. On Via San Remigio at the corner of Via dei Neri the mark from 1966 is simple, while the one from the year 1333 shows the waves of the Arno and a hand with a finger pointing to the high-water line. Its literal translation reads: *November 4, 1333, on the night of Thursday to Friday, the Arno reached this height.*

IL 4 NOVEMBRE 1966 L'ACQUA
D'ARNO ARRIVO A QUEST'ALTEZZA

Address Via San Remigio, corner of Via dei Neri (Santa Croce), 50122 Florence | **Getting there** Bus C1 to the Galleria degli Uffizi stop | **Tip** The monument *Angeli del fango* (Angels of the Mud) stands in the Piazza G. Poggi near the Piazzale Michelangelo.

41 _ Hotel Granduomo
Rubbing shoulders with the Duomo

It was a work of engineering genius! To this day the dome of Santa Maria del Fiore continues to fascinate both experts and laymen. How did Filippo Brunelleschi (1377 – 1446) create it – this gigantic dome with a diameter of about 150 feet – without building load-bearing scaffolding? The museum in the cathedral offers some explanation, but a bit of mystery still remains.

The cathedral's dome is visible from numerous corners of the city. Each time you glimpse it from a different vantage point, it leaves a new impression, but the view from the Hotel Granduomo is particularly unique. Opposite the Duomo, a small doorway right next to the kiosk leads to the front desk of the hotel. About 40 years ago, this entryway did not even exist. It was bricked up and inheritance disputes prevented anyone from gaining access to the building for over a generation.

Today Giuseppe Ancilotti is the sole owner of the hotel. He worked in the fashion industry until his retirement, but today the Granduomo is his passionate pastime. He runs it more like a bed and breakfast, though the nine apartments are on par with those of a boutique hotel, with an unobtrusive staff offering its guests hospitality and privacy.

The staircase is decorated with selected works of art, a potpourri of theatrical costumes, papier-mâché dolls, and art posters. They were chosen by the boss himself, who still browses through the antique shops on Via dei Serragli, in the neighborhood of San Frediano, and always returns with something new.

But it is the extraordinary location of this splendid little hotel that is the real draw. On the roof terrace, where you can sit almost at the height of the top of the dome, you will know you can only be in Florence. The rooms, some of which have small balconies, also offer views of the cathedral.

Address Piazza del Duomo 1/7, 50122 Florence, www.granduomo.com | Getting there
Bus C2 to the Tosinghi stop | Tip On the corner at Via dei Conti 9, you can enjoy a
delicious yet inexpensive menu at La Prova del Nove, a training restaurant for the Saffi
hospitality institute, located in the five-star Hotel Number Nine.

42 Il Bisonte Art Printers
The power of the bison

The only lithograph Pablo Picasso ever produced in Italy was done in 1960, and he had it printed at Il Bisonte Art Printers in Florence. It was just a year after writer and publisher Maria Luigia Guaita joined forces with a group of intellectuals to found Il Bisonte. She had recently returned from Scotland, where she had learned the technique of art engraving.

The signature and logo for Il Bisonte (the bison) were designed by the architect Aristo Ciruzzi: it depicts a bison in the attack position, surrounded by two semicircles, one red and one black. Guaita choose the powerful animal as a symbol, partly because it was one of the first subjects of human painting – such as in the Altamira caves in Spain – and partly because in the culture of the Native Americans, the bison represents female power.

Giò Pomodoro, one of the period's most important abstract artists also numbered among Il Bisonte's first customers. Over the years, his workshop served as a gathering place for avant-garde Italian and international artists of the 20th century, including Pablo Picasso, Jacques Lipchitz, Alexander Calder, Lynn Chadwick, and Henry Moore.

November 4, 1966, the day of the great flood, was – as for many businesses in Florence – a tragic moment in history for the print house. Maria Luigia Guaita was able to save herself by escaping through a window before the floodwaters of the Arno reached her, but many works of art were lost.

Since 1983, Il Bisonte has served as an "International School for Graphic Design," but also continues the tradition of fine art printing. Today, Simone Guaita, nephew of the founder, is president of the foundation. With much enthusiasm, he leads visitors through the rooms full of the tools and works of great artists, recounting stories about them and the rich heritage of printmaking.

Address Via San Niccolò 24r, 50125 Florence, www.ilbisonte.it | Getting there
Bus 23, 13, D to the Poggi stop | Hours Mon–Thu 9am–1pm and 3–7pm, Fri 3–7pm
and by appointment. For guided tours in English, email info@ilbisonte.it | Tip They serve
great appetizers at the bar Il Rifrullo at Via di San Niccolò 55r.

43 In Fabbrica Restaurant
Dining under the hammer and sickle

The room is unadorned, the walls are tiled in green, and small windows look out into the courtyard. After all, it's just the canteen for the Pampaloni factory. The traditional workshop has manufactured silver cutlery, candlesticks, and accessories since 1902. It is famous for its designs with historical motifs and its high quality. Every morning, employees sit in the canteen and have their breakfast together before going into the production hall to pick up their tools.

But in the evenings, this space transforms: It pops off its blue collar and changes into a suit, though still a uniform of sorts, and service begins in the restaurant. The canteen is immersed in classy candlelight, and the heavy chandeliers and tables covered with silver cutlery provide a formal ambiance and a regal flair. Naturally, everything is made out of silver, even the water pitchers. The whole thing feels somewhat surreal when you look up and see the hammer and sickle lit up on the ceiling as a waiter in white gloves serves your appetizer – but it is perfect nonetheless.

This is not a restaurant in a former factory, but in a current one. Francesco and Gianfranco, grandsons of the founder, now run a gourmet eatery in the evenings from the canteen, and employ their workers here as well. They were inspired by Gianfranco's passion for gastronomy and spurred on by the economic crisis. For in hard times, high-quality silver is not in great demand, and their staff needed extra income.

At the helm in the kitchen is the Japanese chef Huigi, who previously worked at the Four Seasons Hotel in Tokyo. Thus there are two menus to choose from, one that is classic Tuscan, and one that is Asian-inspired.

Even if In Fabbrica has garnered some positive gastronomic reviews, you'll still look in vain for a sign. The entrance to the restaurant is the same as for the factory.

Address Via del Gelsomino 99, 50125 Florence, Tel +39/347/5145468, www.pampaloni.com/restaurant | Getting there Bus 11 from Piazza Santa Maria Novella to the Gelsomino 05 stop | Hours Evenings only, closed Mon; reservations strongly recommended | Tip You can also visit the Pampaloni silver factory.

44__The Inverted Balcony

Pitfalls of bureaucracy in the times of the Medici

If you look up as you pass number 12 on the Via Borgo Ognissanti, you will discover a rather peculiar sight: a massive balcony protruding from the palazzo with all of its decorative elements turned upside down. It is a strange building whose origins date back to the 16th century.

At that time, Alessandro de' Medici ruled as the duke of Florence and sought to substantiate his political position through the construction of prestigious buildings, including the Fortezza da Basso. He also introduced city-planning measures that limited the construction of intrusive facades to make the streets appear more spacious. He issued a decree forbidding any architectural elements that were out of proportion with the narrow streets.

The story goes that Messer Baldovinetti, the owner of the palazzo, nonetheless wanted to build an impressive balcony. He was thickheaded, and pressed the authorities to grant him a building permit. Despite being denied repeatedly, he continued to send a new request each and every day. When the duke's patience was finally exhausted, he facetiously replied to Baldovinetti, "The balcony can be built on its head!" He hoped this would discourage the builder once and for all. But Baldovinetti took the official letter literally and built the balcony anyway, installing all of the design features – brackets, scrolls, and balustrades – upside down. Though Alessandro de' Medici was certainly not known to be a pleasant man, he appreciated the humor of Baldovinetti's actions and let the balcony remain.

This anecdote is occasionally criticized among architectural experts, who assert that the palazzo is from the late 16th century and that these quarrels might well have taken place between Grand Duke Ferdinand I and some other Baldovinetti. Embellished or not, it's a good story.

Address Via Borgo Ognissanti 12, 50123 Florence | Getting there Bus C 3 to the Ognissanti stop | Tip At Via Borgo Ognissanti 26, you can admire the landmark building of the Casa-Galleria Vichi by the architect Giovanni Michelazzi.

45 Loggia del Bigallo

The devilish horse

By early morning, the Piazza del Duomo is already teeming with tourists. After all, this is where you can visit one of the most popular sights of the city. But there's also something worth seeing here that visitors rarely know to look for: a richly decorated small palazzo on the large piazza at the corner of Via Cavour.

The Loggia del Bigallo, built in the middle of the 14th century for the so-called Compagnia della Misericordia, or Society of Mercy, became the headquarters of the Compagnia del Bigallo in 1425. On view here in a permanent exhibition are the works of art that were once owned by the company, including the *Crocifisso* (Crucifix) *del Maestro del Bigallo*, the works of Bernardo Daddi and his pupils, and those by Niccolò di Pietro Gerini.

But if you look carefully at the building's facade you will discover a fresco exactly halfway up the building, in which the most conspicuous element is a large black horse. The fresco tells the story of an event that both believers and nonbelievers were taught to fear in the Middle Ages.

In the year 1245, Saint Peter of Verona gave a sermon on the former market square – approximately where the Piazza della Repubblica now stands. The fiery speech was directed against the heretics in the city who did not want to believe or obey the word of God. The event was extremely well attended.

Suddenly, so the legend goes, a black horse appeared in the middle of the crowd and reared up, whinnying. It was believed that none other than the devil himself could have interrupted the preaching of true faith in such a way. The Dominican lifted his hand and made a great sign of the cross. The horse paused for just a moment and fled. When it arrived at the corner of the Palazzo Vecchietti, it vanished. Billows of smoke with the strong odor of sulphur were all that remained.

Address Piazza San Giovanni 1, 50122 Florence | Getting there Bus C 2 to the Oriuolo stop | Tip The oldest depiction of Florence can be seen in the Loggia del Bigallo, open weekdays from 9:30am to 5:30pm.

46 Maharaja of Kolhapur Memorial

In honor of the young Indian prince

In 1870, twenty-one-year-old Rajaram Chuttraputti, the Maharaja of Kolhapur, visited Florence. The Indian ruler had just spent some months studying in England, and planned to take a few days to explore the Tuscan city on his way home. But on November 30, he died suddenly in his hotel room at the Albergo di Piazza Ognisanti.

A repatriation of the body back to Kolhapur was unthinkable at the time, and so the family of the Maharaja began to work through diplomatic channels to bury their son locally according to the rites of his homeland.

Custom dictated that the body of the prince be cremated and his ashes be spread where two rivers meet. The choice fell on the confluence of the River Arno with the Mugnone. The day after his death, at midnight, a pyre was built by his entourage and the body of the young prince was set afire. At dawn, the ashes were placed in a golden urn and given over to the river.

The Maharani Ahilya-Race came to Florence four years later and, as a demonstration of her gratitude, donated 50 pounds sterling to each charitable institution in the city. She also commissioned the English sculptor Carlo Francesco Fuller to build a mausoleum dedicated to the memory of her son: a monument with a canopy under which the bust of the young prince was placed. The memorial tribute was inscribed in four languages: Italian, English, Hindi, and Punjabi.

Today, the monument stands at the end of the Parco delle Cascine, and is the only place in Florence where families are permitted to spread the ashes of their deceased relatives upon the river. The iron bridge that spans over the Arno here – and connects the neighborhoods of Peretola and Isolotto – is named after the monument: Ponte all'Indiano.

Address Piazzale dell'Indiano, 50145 Florence | Getting there Tram 1 from the last stop at Santa Maria Novella Station (Stazione Alamanni), a 5-minute ride to the Cascine station | Tip From here a bike path leads to the Parco Renai, an incredibly beautiful amusement park with a lake (A 10-mile round-trip).

47__The Marzocco
The lion with the shield of lilies

The Piazza della Signoria is one of the city's main attractions, and there are so many sculptures and palazzi to admire that the *Marzocco*, a sandstone lion statue standing four feet tall, is rarely observed. He sits in front of the Palazzo Vecchio and holds the coat of arms of the city of Florence – a shield with a red lily – in his unclenched paw. With a fierce look in his eye he gazes into the distance; after all, it is his job to protect the republic from evil.

The *Marzocco* has served as the symbol of the Florentine Republic since its earliest days in the year 1115 and is intended to represent the power of the people. The name is derived from the Latin word *martius* (also the source for the name of the planet Mars), and it was the Romans who used the lion as a symbol for the city. Real lions were once even kept in Florence, competing in the gladiator fights in the arena. The name of the nearby Via dei Leoni, or Street of the Lions, reminds us today that these great beasts were once held there in cages.

The *Marzocco*, which is the work of the famous sculptor Donatello, dates from the 15th century and is the most magnificent example of the city's symbol located in the piazza. More crest lions can be seen at the Palazzo Vecchio on the top of the tower, at the entrance portal, and on the sides of the building. The statue was commissioned in 1419, the year Pope Martin V visited the city. Originally the proud cat graced the stairs of the papal guest apartment, but later he was moved to the piazza, where he defends his position to this day.

The *Marzocco* in the Piazza della Signoria is a copy of Donatello's original, which can be seen at the Bargello museum.

The heraldic lily is still the symbol with which the municipality of Florence adorns its stationery, and the logo of the soccer club AC Fiorentina (see p. 56) depicts the red lily on a white background.

Address Piazza della Signoria, 50122 Florence | Getting there Bus C 2 to the Condotta stop | Tip On the outside of the church of Orsanmichele on Via dell'Arte della Lana, on the side of Via dei Calzaiuoli, you can admire a splendidly colored example of the Florentine lily in terra-cotta by Luca della Robbia.

48 The Medici Coat of Arms

Six balls: five red and one blue

The iconic coat of arms of the Medici family is emblazoned throughout the city of Florence and, in fact, can be found on practically every cornet in Tuscany. The "balls," in Italian *le palle* (as in English, also the colloquial word for testicles), themselves have an interesting story to tell.

Before the Medici became the undisputed rulers of the city of Florence, the family lived somewhat modestly in Mugello, in the hills north of the city. According to legend, when they came to Florence for the first time, they listed themselves in the registry of doctors and pharmacists as *Medici*, which literally means "doctors" in Italian. The round red balls, which can be seen on the shield, are therefore thought to represent pills, which the Medici manufactured. At that time drugs in pill form were often colored crimson in order to clearly identify them as medication.

The original crest shows only red balls. The number of balls, however, was not always six; in the 14th century it was sometimes eight. Eventually, however, six red balls against a gold background prevailed, according to the schema, 3:2:1. The arrangement later changed to 1:2:2:1, with a slightly larger ball on top.

In the 16th century, one of the red balls was replaced by a blue ball, which depicts the golden lily of the King of France. The Medici had already been granted the honor of using this symbol by Louis XI in 1465, but the princes didn't add the flower motif to their family crest until Caterina de' Medici married the Duke of Orleans. The Pope had arranged the marriage in order to strengthen the alliance between France and the Holy See. When the duke was named King of France in 1547, Caterina became Queen, prompting the Medici to incorporate the lily into their coat of arms.

A particularly fine example can be seen opposite the church in Piazza Ognissanti.

Address Via Borgo Ognissanti 42, 50123 Florence | Getting there Bus C 3 to the Ognissanti stop | Tip You can see *The Last Supper* by Domenico Ghirlandaio in the Ognissanti church.

49 _ The Military Geographic Institute

Exploring the history of Italy through maps

Among the four historically significant libraries in Florence, the Military Geographic Institute is the most impressive. It came into being alongside the Unification of Italy in 1861 through the annexation of the Royal Office of Cartography, which was founded in Naples in 1781.

At that time there were no comprehensive cartographic materials for the newly established Italian state, so, in 1875, the Institute was commissioned to create a detailed topographical map of Italy. It took close to 30 years to complete. About 75 percent of the nation's territory was recorded at a scale of 1:50,000, while areas of significant military interest were done at a scale of 1:25,000. After World War I, the Institute worked until 1927 to record land that had been newly added to the country. Today it is a military facility, headed by a general and tasked with, among other things, supplying the armed forces with up-to-date maps and special military cartographic materials.

The library's monumental hall, originally built in 1694, is adorned with a fresco depicting scenes from the monastic life. The cartographic treasures of the library, with its 12,000 volumes, date mainly from before the Unification. It was only in 1938 that the material was made available to the public.

Today, a collection of 700 atlases spanning from the 16th century to the current day is one of the rarities in the Institute's possession, and some editions can be admired in the reading room. One of the oldest and most valuable volumes is the 1547 *Isolario*, or *Book of Islands*, by Benedetto Bordone. In the museum, you can also view historical instruments for land surveying, such as binoculars, compasses, sextants, and globes.

Address Via C. Battisti 10, 50122 Florence | Getting there Bus 6, 14, 19, 23 to the SS. Annunziata stop | Hours Mon–Fri 8:30am–1pm | Tip Not far away, at Via Camillo Cavour 43, you can admire the impressive reading room in the Marucelliana Library.

50 Mosaics of the Lastrucci Brothers

Stone by stone

It is one of the oldest crafts practiced in the famously artistic city of Florence. Small plates of semiprecious stones such as chalcedony, jasper, lapis lazuli, pearl, and coral are cut with meticulous precision similar to a fretwork, and stone after stone is applied in the desired composition on a supporting plate. The result is a colorful work of art, which radiates just as brilliantly as any painted picture and is also much more durable. This type of stone mosaic, also called Florentine mosaic, dates back to the time of the Medici. The showpiece of this technique is the Cappella dei Principi in San Lorenzo.

The Lastrucci brothers, from the traditionally artisan area of Santa Croce, have practiced their craft for generations. In their showroom one finds a highlight from the household of the Medici family: a sewing box from the Renaissance that once stood in the Palazzo Vecchio. Another historic mosaic piece in the collection is an octagonal table for the Uffizi Gallery, which took ten artisans more than 16 years to create.

Today, the Masters Bruno and Jacopo Lastrucci undertake much more manageable endeavors. Their technique is still exactly the same as it was in the 15th century, but of course the tastes of their 21st-century customers are quite different. With these *pietre dure*, or hard stones, they assemble pictures of birds, fruit, famous celebrities, or landscape scenes, and also make pieces of jewelry. Prices for small works of art such as necklaces, decorative panels, and desktop utensils start at around 200 euros.

The Lastruccis allegedly count among their clients royalty from around Europe. But of course the artists won't name any names. Their company is located in a historic Florentine hospital that has been fully restored. Visitors are always welcome.

Address Via dei Macci 9, 50122 Florence, www.imosaicidilastrucci.it | **Getting there** Bus C2, C3 to the Malborghetto stop | **Hours** Mon–Fri 9am–1pm and 3–7pm | **Tip** You can admire historic works of art in the world-famous Academy of Restoration Work, called Pietre Dure (open Mon–Sat 8:15am–2pm, Thu to 7pm, Via degli Alfani 78, www.opificiodellepietredure.it).

51 Museum of Masonic Symbols

Brothers of the apron

On the second floor of the Museum of Masonic Symbols, the enrollment form of John Wayne is displayed, along with similar documents belonging to writers, poets, and painters who were all Freemasons. An apron worn by George Washington is also exhibited.

The museum is located just a few hundred yards from the place where the first Masonic Lodge in Italy was founded, in 1731. The association still has a considerable number of members, but its reputation has taken a beating in more recent times – especially since the secret lodge P2, with its prominent membership of politicians and generals, filled the press in the 1980s as a hotbed of espionage and corruption.

Nonetheless, the anticlerical Freemasons have often played an important, sometimes even positive, role in Italian history, though the popes repeatedly imposed excommunication against their enlightened members. Masons helped to spread liberal ideas and the principle of religious tolerance through the Italian bourgeoisie. They were also involved in the struggle for Italian unification. Members fought in the resistance against fascism and the Germans.

But there were also Italians who only joined the lodges in order to secure both business and social benefits. This doesn't leave a bad taste in the mouth of museum founder Cristiano Franceschini, however. He himself is a third-generation Freemason. He refers to those members who were the source of the devastating 1980s headlines as "deviants." Throughout his life he has collected ritual objects from the workings of the lodges including aprons of the brothers, magazines, group photos, and film clips from around the world. For 20 years he has curated them into exhibits in the museum, not just for like-minded people, but for anyone interested in the historic order.

Address Via del Orto 7, 50124 Florence, www.musma.firenze.it | Getting there Bus D to the Carmine stop | Hours Daily 3–7pm, Sat and Sun also 10am–1pm | Tip If you prefer something a little less political, on the Piazza de'Nerli you can find excellent *trippa* (tripe), the best in the city according to many Florentines.

52 Osservatorio Ximeniano

The stars over San Lorenzo

If you were to look in the direction of the Duomo from the Piazza San Lorenzo, with its famous Medici chapels, you would discover a green dome among the roofs surrounded by an array of strange antennas. Here, in the heart of the historic city, is the oldest observatory in Florence. It is in use to this day, providing daily weather data.

A large flight of stairs leads up to the entrance of the house at number 6, between shoe and T-shirt vendors. Once at the top, stunning views of San Lorenzo and the Duomo are not all that await visitors, there is also a real treasure of inventions. The Ximeniano has been in existence for 250 years, and over time, a small but exceptional museum has been established.

The observatory was founded in the year 1756 by the Jesuit Father Leonardo Ximenes, who was also an astronomer, mathematician, engineer, and geographer. The weather station owes its name to him. At that time, Jesuits were leaders in the teaching of the natural sciences. At first, the institute dealt primarily with astronomy and hydraulics, but over the course of centuries, it took on other disciplines. Many inventions and works are still preserved here in their original forms. For example, the first seismograph, which was built by Filippo Cecchi and put into operation in 1875, is part of the collection, as is the first map of Tuscany, which impressed the great European powers to such an extent that they regarded the Grand Duchy of Tuscany as an equal.

In 2004 the observatory was converted into a foundation charged with preserving the memory and achievements of the scientists who worked in the institute. A tour is exciting even for those who've never regarded physics as a favorite subject, providing an in-depth look at events in the history of seismology, cartography, astronomy, and meteorology.

Address Piazza San Lorenzo 6, 50123 Florence, Tel +39/055/210420 | Getting there Bus C1 to the Diaz stop | Hours By appointment only; call to make reservations about 1 week prior. Tue, Wed, and Fri 9am – 12pm | Tip You'll get the best view of the observatory from the Trattoria Sergio Gozzi (Piazza di San Lorenzo 8r), along with delicious Tuscan specialties.

53__Piazza della Passera

Where the houses of ill repute once stood

On Borgo San Jacopo, which leads from the Ponte Vecchio in the direction of the Ponte Santa Trinita, the small, narrow Via Toscanella branches off and brings you to an almost idyllic little piazza in the neighborhood of Santo Spirito. At lunchtime, Florentines stop here to grab a panino, and in the evenings at sundown, many meet for drinks and a chat. In the summertime, they hold cultural events in the piazza, including live music and theater festivals.

This square has always been lively, but the name *Piazza della Passera* once conjured up somewhat disreputable images for Florentines. For *passera* is not only the Italian word for a small female sparrow, but in the Italian vernacular it also refers to the female genitals. During the Dark Ages, the piazza was a place known for prostitution and disease. A brothel located here gained great fame over time, and even Cosimo I de Medici was known to have enjoyed its pleasures.

Soon, a second house of ill repute opened just around the corner. The establishment quickly rose to prominence in the city and remained in operation until the 1920s.

When the fascists came to power, the brothel was shut down, and the piazza was renamed Piazza dei Pagoni, for its original name was considered so vulgar it couldn't be tolerated. Pagoni was the name of a family who owned a number of buildings in the neighborhood. On the corner at Via Toscanella, you can still see a sign that reads *Canto d'Pagoni.*

After the fall of the fascist regime and the end of the war, as life slowly returned to normal, the name of the piazza was once more up for discussion. The residents were quick to agree: it should again be called Piazza della Passera. The beautiful and elegant street sign with the pretty blue frame is a good expression of the pride of the community.

Address Piazza della Passera, 50125 Florence | Getting there Bus C3, D to the Pitti stop | Tip You can grab a snack or a panino at the Caffè degli Artigiani (Via dello Sprone 16).

54 Polyphemus
The giant in the former Orti Oricellari

In the competition among stone giants, Michelangelo's *David* has a pretty serious challenger: standing at over 26 feet tall is *Polyphemus*, drinking from a wineskin.

The sculpture dates from 1650 and refers to a famous verse in Homer's *Odyssey*. Polyphemus, the giant with only one eye, was the love child of Poseidon and the sea nymph Thoosa, and was outwitted by Odysseus and his companions, whom he was holding captive. They got him drunk, and as he lay motionless, they burned him in his eye.

The work of art by the master Antonio Novelli stands in what is now the garden of the Victor Hugo French school, but was originally the monumental garden Orti Oricellari. At that time *Polyphemus* was one of many monuments that adorned the garden, including the *Grotta degli Orti*, the *Venti*, and the *Tempio Flora*.

For centuries, the garden belonged to the powerful Rucellai family of Florence. At the end of the 14th century, Bernaro Rucellai had a palazzo built with an open area used to host the meetings of the Accademia Platonica di Firenze. Its members included some of the greatest artists and thinkers of Italy, including Niccolò Machiavelli, who presented his Discorsi – "Thoughts about politics and governance" – there for the first time.

Since the gatherings frequently dealt with political issues, often in favor of a republic and against the unlimited power of the Medici, the meetings were dissolved after several participants were arrested, and the garden fell into neglect.

At the end of the 16th century, it was ironically Bianca Cappello, the second wife of Francesco de Medici, who ordered the restoration of the garden, including new water elements and the integration of the giant *Polyphemus* into the landscape. Today, it is the only part of the original park that can still be seen by the public.

Address Lycee Victor Hugo, Via della Scala 85, 50123 Florence | **Getting there** Tram T1, Bus 37, to the Stazione Alamanni and Alamanni 5 stop | **Hours** School garden: Wed 2–4:30pm | **Tip** The Giardini Corsini, just around the corner at Via del Prato 58, is also worth a visit.

55 The Roster Greenhouse
The history of the Crystal Palace

When engineer Giacomo Roster was entrusted with the construction of a heated greenhouse for exotic plants to be used during the national horticultural exhibition in Florence, he took great inspiration from innovative architect and botanist Joseph Paxton, who designed the exhibition building for the first World's Fair in London in 1851. His resulting work in glass and iron was similar to the Crystal Palace in Hyde Park, after which it was nicknamed.

Roster's "crystal palace" was inaugurated in 1880 and boasted impressive proportions (it is still the largest greenhouse in Italy). Its area measures 126 by 56 feet – in total nearly 7,000 square feet – and the roof height measures nearly 46 feet. It looks like the over-turned hull of a ship, and was built using a wood frame construction technique. The glass surfaces are made up of many transparent plates that are slightly layered over each other, so that the rain can run off as it does on roof tiles. The 24 load-bearing pillars are adorned with decorative cast iron.

In the beginning, the impressive building in the middle of the botanical gardens was also used for exhibitions and events. But after its initial heyday, it was unfortunately left to decay.

Since 1930, the greenhouse has belonged to the city of Florence and been open to the public. Beginning at the turn of the millennium, however, it underwent a nearly €1 million restoration. At the rededication ceremony in 2010, then mayor of Florence and current Italian prime minister Matteo Renzi called it "a magical place in the center of Florence."

View the greenhouse at its most beautiful by sitting outside with an aperitif on a balmy summer night in the city (open until midnight, www.giardinoartecultura.it). During sunset, the glass structure appears immersed in fantastic colors, like something out of a fairy tale.

Address Via Vittoria Emanuelle II 17, 50139 Florence | Getting there Bus 12 to the Puccinotti, Farmacia Notari stop | Hours Jan–Mar 8:30am–6pm; Apr–May 8:30am–7pm; June–Aug 8:30am–8pm; Oct–Dec 8:30am–6pm | Tip Those who use the entrance at Via Trento 5, called *del Parnaso*, will meet the "dragon" in *Il Giardino degli Orti del Parnaso*, reminiscent of the work of Gaudì.

56 — The Signs of Clet Abraham
Angels and devils guiding the way

Imbrattamento, which literally means "contamination" in English, is the legal charge that has been leveled against the no longer anonymous "urban sticker artist" in the Tuscan city of Pistoia. In Florence, too, a small dossier against him already lies atop the judges' table.

Clet Abraham has literally redesigned the region's road signs in a much more colorful and imaginative way. Prohibition signs now feature an angel, warning signs depict the nose of Pinocchio, and a traffic sign shows a gentleman picking flowers. "The street signs in the city are basically a command, so I have tried to make the information more positive. Rather than 'contaminating' the signs with my stickers, I am making them more beautiful." Whether or not the €500 fine from the municipality of Pistoia becomes final, Pistoia, Florence, and other cities throughout Tuscany are now full of Clet's modified street signs.

Abraham boasts quite a large fan base in Florence and in several other cities in Europe, and versions of his signs can be enjoyed in Berlin, Rome, Milan, London, and Paris.

On the Ponte alle Grazie in Florence, a life-size bronze statue appeared to walk weightless above the waters of the Arno for more than a year. Clet did not seek permission for this piece either, yet it still managed to linger in its place.

Abraham always works at night to avoid scrutiny, and by early morning, signs may sport an angel face or devil horns. To the right, you might see a signpost decorated with a euro, a reference to capital, while over to the left a sign dons a heart, thus going in a more "social" direction. In any case, the works of Clet Abraham make a political statement.

Since 2006, the French-born artist has lived and worked in Florence, where he has his own studio and sells his sculptures and paintings.

Address Atelier Clet Abraham, Via dell'Olmo 8r, San Niccolò, 50125 Florence | **Getting there** Bus 6, 23 to the Ponte alle Grazie stop | **Tip** Excellent Florentine cuisine is served right next door to Abraham's studio at the Osteria Antica Mescita San Niccolò, Via di San Niccolò 60r. Especially spectacular are the rooms in the basement from an old crypt that dates back to the year 1000. (www.osteriasanniccolo.it).

57 __ The Stone of Shame

Rubbernecking in the Middle Ages

Tourists flock to the Loggia del Mercato Nuovo, just behind the Piazza della Signoria, to rub the nose of the famous *Porcellino* ("piglet") because it is said to bring good luck.

But in the hustle and bustle of the busy market, there is another, less uplifting, attraction that often goes unnoticed. Just about at the center of the loggia, you'll find a large round marble mosaic on the ground, which dates back to a ruthless practice from the Middle Ages. It represents the wheel of a *carroccio* in actual size. These carts served as a sort of "home on wheels" for the medieval Italian republic during wartime. The city's flag and an altar were carried atop a rectangular platform. Before heading out into battle, the soldiers gathered around the cart, and a priest prayed to the Lord for victory.

This very place, where the Florentines once displayed their pride – and which the wheel still symbolizes today – is also where the supreme court in Florence, housed at that time nearby in the Palazzo del Bargello, chose to publicly humiliate offenders.

The marketplace, being the center of city life in the Middle Ages, was full of vendors, customers, and passersby, guaranteeing an audience for the scammers, counterfeiters, and debtors who were dragged here at lunchtime.

Court guards stripped the criminals from the waist down, bound their arms and legs, and pulled them with leashes to this spot. They then beat their naked backsides repeatedly before the crowds. Since then, the marble circle has been referred to as the *Pietra dello Scandalo*, or the Stone of Shame.

Public punishment and humiliation carried other serious consequences for those tormented. At the very least, they could not resume work in their professions or trades, and in the worst cases, they had to move to other neighborhoods or leave the city altogether.

Address Piazza del Mercato Nuovo, 50123 Florence | Getting there Bus C2 to the Porta Rossa stop | Tip Leather bags and belts are sold at the market at reasonable prices.

58_ The Stork Room in La Specola

A symbiosis of art and science

Pietro Leopoldo of Lorraine – who would become Emperor Leopold II and rule the Grand Duchy of Tuscany after the Medici – was inspired by the Enlightenment to open the cabinet of curiosities of the Medici to the public. Alongside artistic treasures, they had amassed a substantial collection of specimens from nature, including fossils, minerals, exotic plants, and animals, including an elephant who died in Florence. All of these sciences – from the collection of minerals under the earth and up to the heavens and astronomy – are housed in La Specola.

Officially opened in 1775, La Specola remained the world's only science museum until the beginning of the 19th century, bringing together under one roof research in the sciences, arts, literature, and philosophy. And on its top floor is the Torrino, an astrological observatory more than 130 feet high above the city, still equipped with the instruments of Galileo Galilei (1564–1642).

Beneath the octagonal observatory, in its own hall, is the pride of Florence: the unique solar clock used for measuring the passing of the sun over the local meridian, hence the name Meridian Room. Also called the "Stork Room" for the pairs of sculpted storks in midflight that decorate its columns, the beautiful, atmospheric hall with its ray of sunlight is a prime example of the confluence of art and science.

Giuseppe Antonio Slop, astronomer and lecturer (1740–1808), designed the room and chose the image of stork, as it symbolizes conscientiousness. The two columns are located on the same north-south axis used by the birds when they migrate. On the marble sundial in the floor, decorated with ornate symbols of the zodiac, you can locate the exact solar noon.

Address Via Romana 17, 50125 Florence, Tel +39/055/2756444, www.msn.unifi.it,
edu@msn.unifi.it | **Getting there** Bus 11, 36 to the San Felice stop | **Hours** Mon–Fri
9am–5pm, Sat 9am–1pm; visit the Torrino on special occasions, or any other time, upon
request by email or phone | **Tip** For more than 50 years, the Trattoria La Casalinga at Via
dei Michelozzi 9r (open Mon–Sat 12–2:30pm and 7–10pm) has served delicious, simple
Tuscan dishes like *ribollita* (a cooked soup with cabbage) or *pasta e ceci* (pasta with
chickpeas).

59 Studio d'Arte Valkama

The fresco rescuer

Those who make their way to Florence on a voyage of discovery will come face-to-face with this centuries-old painting technique almost everywhere: frescoes, painted with water-soluble pigments on fresh limestone plaster, create boundless breadth and carry the viewer into an imaginary time and space. Frescoes can be seen in the church of Santa Maria Novella, in San Marco, and in the Brancacci Chapel. But it was not only in public buildings that rooms were decorated with frescoes; the walls in the palazzi were also adorned with these colorful murals.

By the 1970s, however, many did not want to see the small angels and saints in their private homes and whitewashed them unceremoniously with cheap paint until there was nothing left to see. In these cases, Tamara Valkama comes to the rescue. The artist, born in Stockholm and an alumna of the Academy of Fine Arts of Florence, works as a restorer and specializes in decorative works. She can paint a floor to look like marble or hardwood, so that it is visually indistinguishable from the real thing.

But Valkama's greatest satisfaction comes from restoring frescoes. Once she found – under many layers of paint – a motif depicting the mythical love story between the god Cupid and the mortal princess Psyche. Restoring such a work is an extremely delicate undertaking. Valkama's challenge is always to make everything as visibly close to the original as possible. The less there is to see, the more restrained she must be with her colors. And everything she does must always be carried out in a way that can be reversed, in the event that materials later become available that might provide a better quality of reconstruction.

In Valkama's own original work, there are no angels or saints in the spotlight; the subject of her last series was jellyfish. It can be viewed in her studio.

Address Piazza Piattellina 3, 50124 Florence, www.tamarabvalkama.it, tbastiani@yahoo.it | **Getting there** Bus D to the Carmine stop | **Hours** To arrange a visit, it is best to email the artist directly | **Tip** Valkama offers courses in fresco painting, in which she teaches basic skills involving the use of different materials, colors, and painting techniques.

60__ The Tabernacle on Via dei Pepi

George and the dragon

Today most people just hurry past Florence's tabernacles; many Florentines themselves barely notice them. There are over 1,200 of these inconspicuous works of art adorning the city's street corners. A fairly common motif is of the Madonna and Child.

During the Christianization of the city, many temples and altars with deities were built on corners (which were regarded by those of the Christian faith as entrances to the underworld) in order to protect the roads and their travelers.

Since the year 1200, a struggle between Roman Catholics and nonbelievers has raged in the city, played out in public sermons and also in the religious imagery displayed on many facades and public buildings. In the 14th century, the portraits functioned as altars, and after mass, candles and lights were lit that would bear witness to the "true faith" – and also serve as streetlamps. From the 15th century, guilds, monasteries, religious communities, and private citizens began to commission famous artists to create images for their tabernacles, which were a testament to their faith – not to mention their power and wealth. After World War II, historians and researchers took a particular interest in the tabernacles, and, since 1950, many have been restored.

The tabernacle at the Canto di Sant'Anna was once decorated with the Madonna and Child along with saints Domenico and Francesco, and two coats of arms. Its remains were badly damaged in the great flood of 1966. In its place, a young artist created a 1980s-style portrait called *Saint George and the Dragon*, which is the most unusual work of art among the tabernacles of the city. Steeped in legend, the martyr's saintly image is one of the most well known in Christendom.

Address Via dei Pepi / Via dei Pilastri, 50121 Florence | **Getting there** Bus 14, 23, C1, C2 to the Salvemini stop | **Tip** The most important of the tabernacles is the *Tabernacolo delle Fonticine* at the corner of Via Nazionale and Via del Ariento, with its putti spitting water and a Madonna by the artist della Robbia.

61__ The Tower of Santa Maria Maggiore

Berta's watching you from above

Every day thousands of tourists walk along on the road from the train station to the Duomo without pausing to notice the simple Romanesque church that stands on the Via de'Cerretani at the corner of Piazza Santa Maria Maggiore. But as you look up, you'll be surprised to discover the head of a woman carved in marble with combed-back curls protruding from the medieval stones of the tower.

Two legends swirl around her stony face: The astrologer, alchemist, physician, and poet Francesco Stabili was, as was not uncommon in 1327, accused of witchcraft and sentenced to death. A woman named Berta heard the convicted man call out for water from the window of the tower. Convinced that the offender had made a pact with the devil, she refused the wizard's request: "If you drink water, you will no longer burn," she told him. To which he is said to have replied, "And you will no longer move your head from this spot." And so it was.

In another legend that is often retold, Berta is instead a green-grocer who spent her entire life on the Via de'Cerretani peddling her produce, which she grew outside the gates of the city. One day she became fed up with not knowing exactly when the gates would be closed – and thus when she would have to make her way back out into the fields. So she decided to donate a bell to the church that would be rung with the closing of the gates every day. In recognition of Berta, the Florentines created the marble head.

Less exciting is the cultural and historical explanation: the marble head is a fragment that was used to beautify the facade of many Romanesque buildings. No matter the background, Florentines nonetheless refer to her simply as "Berta."

Address Piazza di Santa Maria Maggiore, 50123 Florence | **Getting there** Bus C 2 to the Olio stop | **Tip** You can enjoy a glass of wine in the Fiaschetteria Nuvoli Piazza dell'Olio, actually a wine cellar, open daily from 9:30am – 9pm, or a snack until 4:30pm (ham, salami, and crostini, among other items)

62 __ The Vasari Corridor

Panoramic windows for Hitler

The tourists fight their way through the crowds on the Ponte Vecchio, but in the passageway above, there is a majestic calm. It was the same in the time of Cosimo I de' Medici, called Cosimo the Great. The corridor connected the Palazzo Vecchio, his workplace, to the Palazzo Pitti, his residence, and he was able to pass between them unbothered by the people. At that time, the Ponte Vecchio was filled with butcher shops, making it difficult to cross. In 1564, the architect Giorgio Vasari created the pathway across the rooftops of the shops, affording the prince both privacy and safety.

Four centuries later, on May 9, 1938, the Vasari Corridor became one of the highlights of Hitler's visit to Italy.

Mussolini had hired high-profile art experts, among them the archaeologist Ranuccio Bianchi Bandinelli, an anti-fascist. The Italian dictator was dependent on these scholars, however, to help him hold his own against his art-loving German allies. The scholars led Mussolini and Hitler, along with Ribbentrop, Goebbels, Himmler, and Hess, through the collections of the Palazzo Pitti, and from there, through the Vasari Corridor.

Until that time, the view down into the streets had been through barred porthole windows. But for the occasion of Hitler's visit, the Duce had panoramic windows built over the center of the Ponte Vecchio. It is believed today that Hitler was so impressed by the design that he spared the bridge during the German bombing of Florence.

The Vasari Corridor is a gem for art lovers. Around 1,000 artists' self-portraits, including those by Tintoretto, Rembrandt, and Chagall, decorate the walkway.

You exit the corridor through a rather inconspicuous door and emerge quite abruptly before the beautifully kitschy statued grotto by Bernardo Buontalenti in the Boboli Gardens.

Address Piazza della Signoria, 50122 Florence | Getting there Bus C 2 to the Condotta stop | Hours By guided tour only. Order tickets through the Polo Fiorentino Museale, Tel +39/055/294883, www.polomuseale.firenze.it, or through a private agency such as www.florencetown.com (about €80) | Tip The Galileo Museum, located nearby in an old palace, is filled with fascinating historical objects (Piazza dei Giudici 1, open daily 9:30am–6pm, Wed to 1pm, www.museogalileo.it).

63 Villa Broggi-Caraceni

Art Nouveau in the city of the Renaissance

Visitors to Florence on the trail of the Renaissance can easily pass from highlight to highlight. Less known, however, are the few original works in the Liberty style, the Italian iteration of the artistic movement that is known in other countries as Art Nouveau. A true example of this style is the Villa Broggi-Caraceni, named for its first owner.

To admire the exterior of the elegant building, you'll have to make the trek out into the suburbs to one of the neighborhoods that emerged in the 20th century, made up for the most part of two-story cottages built for the upper middle class. Many of these so-called *villini* are quite remarkable interpretations of various modern architectural styles. The Villa Broggi-Caraceni, located near the Piazza Beccaria, is the most important work by the architect Giovanni Michelazzi (1879–1920), aside from the Casa Emporio, a rowhouse in the Ognissanti District.

Michelazzi designed the villa between 1910 and 1911 in collaboration with Galileo Chini (1873–1956), a Tuscan designer, ceramist, painter, and renowned artist who taught at the Academy of Fine Arts in Florence.

The structure is octagonal in shape with a tower and a loggia. The loggia's decorative elements are ceramic, and its railing is wrought iron. A small balcony adorns its east side. The interior is situated around a central staircase with a dome-shaped skylight sporting a lantern made of colored glass with decorations in wrought iron, reminiscent of the shape of a spider. On the dome, you'll see dancing women painted by Chini.

As the only Art Nouveau villa in Florence, the building has been preserved in its original condition, both inside and out. Though not accessible to the public, the interior contains period paintings, stained glass, mosaic floors, and stone vases.

Address Via Scipione Ammirato 99, 50136 Florence | Getting there Bus 8, 12, 13, 14, 23 to the Beccaria stop | Hours Not open to the public | Tip Many fantastic sweet treats await you in Dolce e Dolcezze, located at Piazza Beccaria 8r (closed Mon)

64_ Villa Castello

Separating the wheat from the chaff

The charming garden of the Villa Castello was once used by the Medici to host important gatherings. They invited young ladies here from the aristocratic houses of Europe in order to introduce them to their sons as potential wives. The women also allegedly served as muses for Botticelli, who was inspired in the garden to paint his world-famous *Birth of Venus*.

The villa, which is now a World Heritage Site, is not freely accessible to the public. It is the seat of the Crusca, the Italian academy of linguistics. On a guided tour, you'll discover not only frescoes from the school of Ghirlandaio, but will also learn of the remarkable history of the academy, which published the first dictionary of the Italian language in 1612.

Accademia della Crusca translates into English as the "Academy of Bran." It was founded in Florence in 1583 by five writers who met for social gatherings, jokingly referred to as the *cruscate*. Their aim was to clean up the Italian language, or to "separate the wheat from the chaff," so to speak. They considered the linguistic ideal at that time to be the works of the great poets Dante, Petrarch, and Boccaccio.

More than 100 wooden paddles hang on the walls of the villa's great hall – similar to peels used to remove bread from the oven – decorated with impressive symbols and sayings. Every new member of the Accademia had to introduce himself with a unique motto. They all came up with dictums that had to do with the theme of flour and bread – the flour mill is the symbol of the Accademia. Some of the most successful sayings cited the poet Petrarch, who in one quote presented himself as the *infarinato*, or the "floured," and in another the *lievitato*, or "he who rises," by which he meant that his language would lift you up – a bit of 16th-century-self-marketing.

Address Via di Castello 46, 50141 Florence | Getting there Take Bus 2 or 28 from the train station to the Via Sestese 5 stop, then turn right at the traffic light onto Via Giuglio and follow it until you reach the villa | Hours Tours offered the last Sun of the month hourly beginning at 10am. For an English-speaking guide, email accademiadellacrusca@cscsigma.it | Tip The Medici Villa La Petraia with its romantic park at Via Petraia 40 is just a five-minute walk away.

65__Villa Favard
Titans of botany

The oak tree in the Parco delle Cascine is four times taller than Michelangelo's *David*. The 140-year-old Lebanese cedar in the Villa Fabbricotti reached a height of nearly 80 feet. In Florence, there are a total of 13 giant trees that are protected under law. Anyone who inflicts damage on one of these Goliaths risks a 100,000-euro fine. Seven of them are publicly accessible, while the other six stand in private parks.

The most beautiful place to get to know some of these botanical skyscrapers is at the Villa Favard in the Rovezzano neighborhood, in the south of Florence. The villa originally dates back to the 15th century, but the Baroness Fiorella Favard de l'Anglade turned it into a cultural meeting place in 1857 and had the extensive gardens re-landscaped. She included exotic varieties of trees such as Lebanon cedars, although the first of these was actually planted much earlier, in the 1600s.

The city of Florence has owned the villa since the 1970s. But even many Florentines are not aware of the villa's parklands. A walk through the meadows on its lanes lined with lemon trees is truly wonderful. Take a seat on a bench and enjoy the ambiance and the free concert coming from the classrooms of the conservatory that has been housed in the villa for some years.

The oldest Lebanese cedar, which was imported from Lebanon in the 17th century, has a trunk so large in diameter that your arms won't reach all the way around it. Some of the other trees have a glorious, but also tragic, history. Two of them stand along the alley among the linden trees. You'll see cuts at the bottom of one of them, which stem from the year 1944, when German troops hid their vehicles under the trees to avoid being spotted by the Allied air forces. Another one was nearly decapitated – that is to say, it was struck by lightning.

Address Villa Favard, Via Aretina 511, 50136 Florence | **Getting there** Bus 14, 14 A from the train station to the Rovenzzano V stop | **Hours** Jun, Jul, Aug 8am–8pm, otherwise 9am–6pm | **Tip** The sculpture park of the artist Enzo Pazzagli is nearby at Via Sant'Andrea a Rovvezzano 5 (www.pazzagli.com).

66__Villa Fontallerta
The lightness of being

"Open, Sesame!" Recite this secret password, and the heavy iron gates will slowly swing to the side. An avenue lined with olive groves will lead you through a romantic park, slightly fragrant with spices. It will take you a bit of time to reach the villa, and every now and then along the way, you'll catch a glimpse of a fantastic view over Florence. Outside the main entrance, waiting to greet you, will be Anna Rasponi, heir to the Gaddi family of hoteliers from Rome, who relocated to the city on the Arno when Florence briefly served as the capital of Italy in 1865.

Villa Fontallerta was originally built in the 13th century. The Gaddis turned it into a meeting place for the nobility and for those interested in culture, transforming its appearance into what you see today.

Upon entering the villa, you'll pass first through a gallery of family portraits. "We call them the wigs," jokes Signora Rasponi, because the truth is that nobody knows for sure exactly who is depicted. In the loggia, you'll discover a Madonna by Della Robbia, from the workshop of the famous Florentine family of sculptors.

"Oh, it's not so big in here," muses Anna Rasponi, although the great hall, which was once the winter garden, would make an excellent setting for the Viennese Opera Ball. Somehow the antique furniture, frescoed ceilings, and coats of arms on the walls do not make the villa feel dark or oppressive – rather, it exudes a certain lightness. Perhaps this uplifting atmosphere has always existed, and that's the reason why Boccaccio set one of the tales from his *The Decameron* here: the cheerful, frivolous story about the romance between the painter Calandrino and the beautiful Niccolosa.

The ultimate highlight is the villa's bird room, completely covered with frescoes from the 16th century, attributed to Bernardino Poccetti.

Address Viale Augusto Righi 50, 50137 Florence | Getting there Bus 11 (from Piazza San Marco) to the Salvatino stop | Hours By appointment. Contact Anna Rasponi, Tel +39/055/573911, annarasponi@gmail.com | Tip The hostel Europa Villa Camerata at Viale Augusto Righi 4 is housed in a villa (www.ostellofirenze.it).

67__Villoresi's Studio

Perfumer to the stars

Ring the doorbell marked *Villoresi* and over the intercom you'll hear the instruction: *"Ultimo piano"* (top floor). Now just take the elevator to the 4th floor, walk up a few steep steps, and you'll find yourself in the middle of the workshop of the alchemist of fragrances: Lorenzo Villoresi.

The space is filled with 10,000 noble bottles of essences. A Caucasian carpet covers the floor, and a portrait of Villoresi's grandmother – a rather resolute-looking woman – decorates the wall. There is also a comfortable antique sofa and an armchair. A unique and lovely view over the Arno and the city opens directly out from the loggia.

Villoresi's studio is located in the old villa of his family, and he has been creating his extravagant fragrances here since 1990. Many celebrities have sat at the large 17th-century table: film director Ridley Scott, fashion icon Jacqueline Kennedy, and model Linda Evangelista, to name a few. All of them asked the master to compose their own personal scents. A small bottle from this world of imagination and exoticism costs about 3,600 euros.

The learned philosopher and philologist discovered his passion while traveling for his studies, particularly along the Silk Road – then, as now, a mecca for lovers of rare spices and herbs. Back home, he began to experiment and create. In doing so, he continued in the tradition of an old Florentine specialty. In the 15th century the art of perfumery was greatly celebrated, thanks to the future queen of France, Caterina de' Medici. She took her perfumer, Renato Bianco, with her to Paris, where he became renowned as "René le Florentin."

The most prominent components of Villoresi's creations are essential oils and extracts from around the world, combined with Tuscan ingredients such as olive and cypress. Villoresi is now transforming another palazzo into his "Fragrance Academy."

Address Via dei Bardi 14, 50125 Florence | Getting there C 3 bus to the Mozzi stop | Hours Studio: Mon – Sat 10am – 7pm | Tip Visit the Giardino Bardini, with its many fragrant plants and ancient water channels. The entrance is at Costa San Giorgio 2 (Dec – Feb, daily 8:15am – 4:30pm, June – Aug, daily 8:15am – 7:30pm, Sep – Nov and Mar – May, daily 8:15am – 5:30pm).

68 __ Cheese Throwing
The ancient sport of shepherds

In the sport of cheese throwing, the choice of wheel can make the difference between victory and defeat. A different shape and size suits each competitor, depending on their particular technique. In any case, the cheese should be well aged; Parmesan is a good choice, or perhaps a Sardinian Pecorino. In general, the wheels will weigh between 22 and 33 pounds, but boulders up to about 66 pounds are not unheard of. The track is nearly 1,000 feet long. The competition's aim: he who catapults the cheese the farthest along the track wins. The cheese cannot leave the track or break apart. It sounds easy, but try just one trial roll and you will see that this requires quite a bit of practice and strength.

The *tricciòlo* – basically a strap – is the main tool that wraps around the cheese and helps to propel it, and this is attached to the thrower's wrist with a loop. A piece of wood, called the brigliòlo, holds the strap before starting. The thrower uses his momentum to swing his arms around, the strap is released, and the cheese starts to roll.

Cheese tossing has been practiced since the time of the Etruscans, and wall murals, such as in Tarquinia, depict the pastime. Competitions are held all over Italy, and every April, Gallicano is the venue for the national championship.

The sport has always been a part of the everyday lives of shepherds. For centuries, athletes competed on village streets to the enthusiastic shouts of onlookers – much to the annoyance of the local residents. Thus official prohibitions can be found in the bylaws of certain communities. But the rules of the sport are now codified by the Italian Olympic Committee.

Cheese throwing is practiced all year long in the Circolo il Barchetto in Gallicano, and the public can watch on Sundays. The track is out in the open, beside a small lake with mountains in the background.

Address Via Serchio 17, Loc. La Spiaggia, 55027 Gallicano | **Getting there** From Barga take the SP 7 toward Fornaci di Barga; about 100 yards past the sign for Pian di Coreglia, turn right at the intersection and cross the Servchio River, then go right, and after about 500 yards turn right again, onto Via Serchio. The Circolo will be across the street. | **Tip** The Ristorante Pizzeria Il Barchetto is located across from Circolo.

69 The Ferrucci Monument

"Coward, you kill a dead man!"

Only the church bells break the silence in these parts, every quarter hour, half hour, and on the hour. Other than that, all is quiet in the idyllic medieval village 2,690 feet up in the Pistoia Mountains. Sitting on the sunny side of the Apennines along the route to Abetone, the ski resort for the Florentines, Gavinana tends to attract more visitors in winter.

In the middle of the village square, next to the 12th-century church of Santa Maria Assunta, stands the proud equestrian statue of Captain Francesco Ferrucci, also called Ferruccio. At its dedication ceremony in 1920 (the Florentine sculptor Emilio Gallori had been working on the statue since 1913), the mayor was joined by many political dignitaries because Ferrucci was considered a national hero. He died on August 3, 1530, in the bloody battle between the troops of Emperor Charles V and the Florentine militia. The battle marked a turning point in the history of Tuscany, paving the way for the return of the Medici family and Duke Cosimo I, who again came to power in the middle of the 16th century, thanks to Pope Clement VII.

Ferrucci became a mythical hero. Fighting for republican ideals and the independence of the princes, he was the embodiment of boldness, in contrast to his treacherous and cowardly murderer. "Coward, you kill a dead man!" Ferrucci allegedly called out as his last words, just before Fabrizio Maramaldo, an Italian in the service of the emperor, slayed him with a knife while the captain lay injured and defenseless on the ground.

The myth surrounding Ferrucci was already celebrated during the Risorgimento, the national Unification movement, and also after the 1861 Unification was complete. His name even found its way into the Italian national anthem by Goffredo Mameli: "From Ferruccio has every man / The heart and the hand."

Address Piazza Francesco Ferrucci, Gavinana, 51028 San Marcello Pistoiese | **Getting there** Take the SR 66 Pistoiese, halfway between Pistoia and Abetone, and turn right at the Passo dell'Oppio; after about two miles you'll reach Gavinana | **Tip** The story of the hero is documented in the Ferrucci Museum (open Jan–Jun and Sept–Dec, Wed–Sun 10am–6pm, Jul and Aug 10am–7pm).

70__Tizzone, the Black Salami

The "Brunello" of sausages

The recipe for Tizzone dates back to an old tradition in Versilia from the late 18th century. Carrara marble has been mined in this region on the northwest edge of Tuscany since ancient times. The workers in the quarries needed good, hearty food that would keep them full and well nourished for long stretches of time.

Only the best cuts of pork, that is to say the shoulder, ham, and parts of the back, are mixed by hand and combined with mountain herbs to make this salami. For today's producers, it is important that the meat used is from free-range animals – under no circumstances can it come from a factory farm, which would make the water content too high and interfere with the maturation process. Once in its casing, the salami is first stored in a cellar for three months. For the next stage, vast amounts of wood chips are slowly heated in a huge oven until they glow red hot and then are cooled back down. The salami is then laid in the ashes, where it can stay for up to nine months. This is what gives the Tizzone its black coating.

A salami that weighs about eight to eleven pounds is declared *Riserva*. Thanks to the long aging process, the *Riserva* salami is more intense. This category, whose nomenclature was borrowed from the wine industry, signals its high quality. But ultimately – tradition or not – it is the taste that is most important: Tizzone melts in your mouth, which can hardly be said for all types of salami. This black salami is produced exclusively in Giustagnana, in the hinterland of Forte dei Marmi. This community of only 140 people lies high in the mountains overlooking the sea, and is surrounded by the quarries where Michelangelo personally chose his marble. In the village's small family-run shops, they offer samples of the Tizzone they have for sale, along with other regional specialties.

Address Azienda Agricola Felice Lorenzoni Loc. Colle di Nagni, 55047 Giustagnana, Seravezza | Getting there From Forte dei Marmi take the SP 68/SP 9 toward Seravezza, Guistiniana in the Apuan Alps | Tip Azienda Agricola owns an *agriturismo* with rustic apartments in the village (www.aziendalorenzoni.com).

71 Castello dell'Aquila

The knight's castle

When Signora Gabriella Girandin bought this property, it was a ruin high on the mountain with breathtaking views – the perfect place to find some peace and quiet. During the restoration work on the property, however, the new owners happened upon numerous objects from the Middle Ages. Experts finally discovered that on this spot once stood the castle of the noble Italian Malaspina family, who originally came from Lombardy and held the margravate of Massa and Carrara in the province of Lunigiana in the north of Tuscany during the 14th century.

Even today, just one glance up is enough to understand the strategic importance of the castle: the view sweeps far out into the country – from up here one could control the entire area.

The restoration work cost billions and lasted about 10 years. Individual sections that had been destroyed were rebuilt in a manner faithful to the original construction, and today the castle is a magnificent work of medieval architecture. The rooms are equipped with all the modern conveniences, including heat, so that paying guests can stay the night in the castle. The panoramic terrace offers visitors a breathtaking view of the highest peaks of the Apuan Alps, including the Pizzo d'Uccello at 5,843 feet.

The castle's chapel was restored and consecrated again in 2005. The only preserved fresco of the castle is located here. Most of its other art objects have fallen victim to looters.

In 2004, a skeleton was also discovered among all the debris. It turned out to belong to a knight from the 14th century: a crossbow arrow had pierced his throat and had then come out through his cervical vertebrae. The knight was the subject of several theses and has since become famous among anthropologists and forensic scientists. At the castle an exact replica has since taken the skeleton's place at the site where it was found.

Address Castello dell'Aquila, Via del Castello, 54013 Gragnola, Tel +39/058599157 or 335/6628357, www.castellodellaquila.it | Getting there Take the A 12 to the Aulla exit, then follow the SS 63 in the direction of Fivizzano-Reggio Emilia. Five miles before Fivizzano, take a right toward Gragnola-Gassano-Equi Terme, and in Gassano follow signs to the Castelo d'Aquila (the last portion of the road is unpaved). | Hours Open year-round, guided tours by appointment | Tip In nearby Casola, in Lunigiana, you can have a very exclusive vacation at the villa Casa della Quercia, with its private pool surrounded by the mountains (www.casadellaquercia.com).

72___Fonte della Fata Morgana
The fountain of youth

No sooner have you left behind the houses of the village of Grassina, about 10 miles outside of Florence, than you'll be welcomed by a lush rolling landscape full of fields and olive trees. Around a bend, a bright pink cottage appears in the middle of the greenery like something truly out of this world – the fairy house known as the Casa delle Fate.

Magical powers were once attributed to the spot. The fountain, which at one time bubbled vigorously, allegedly made man's ultimate dream come true: it was said that those who drank from it would never age. At least this is what the landlord, Bernardo Vecchietti, believed when he had the building constructed on the grounds of his summer home, Villa di Riposo, or the Villa of Relaxation, in the second half of the 16th century. According to many experts, the cottage was designed by the Flemish sculptor Giambologna, who had strong support from his patron. He created a unique example of garden architecture, something that appears to be a cross between a fountain house and a grotto – there's just nothing else like it.

Inside, you'll find the aforementioned fountain, from which the marble statue *Fata Morgana*, by Giambologna, once rose. The statue, named after Morgan Le Fay from the legend of King Arthur, lends its title to the place. The cottage is richly decorated with architectural details, and the artist was probably inspired by the exquisite nature all around him, which seems to exude a special kind of enchantment of its own.

Mystical stories and legends of nymphs and fairylike creatures who suddenly appeared on warm summer nights are one reason for the exuberance of the summer festivals held on the grounds by the illustrious Vecchietti family from Florence.

And even if today nobody believes the story about the charmed water, the magic of the place remains, fairies or not.

Address Via di Fattucchia, 50012 Grassina, Bagno a Ripoli | Getting there Bus 31 or 32 from Piazza San Marco to the Grassina stop, from Piazza di Grassina right through the village to the intersection, then right on Via delle Fonti and follow signs towards Agriturismo Bottaia (from here about a 30-minute walk). | Hours Call to make a reservation a few days prior, Tel +39/3355428515; Signora Tucci from the municipality of Bagno a Ripoli will come and open the fairy cottage. | Tip There is a lovely *agriturismo* called Borgo Bottaia at Via delle Fonti 62 (www.borgobottaia.it).

73 __ Carbone, the Terra-cotta Artist

Apprentice to "the last Etruscan"

First the Etruscans, and later the Romans, used the high-quality clay from the region around Impruneta to make vases and amphorae to store wine, oil, and other products. The earth there is particularly rich in iron and copper, which makes the vessels uniquely hardy, and guarantees protection from frost and salty air. The master Brunelleschi himself utilized roof tiles manufactured in Impruneta for the Duomo in Florence, for only the best was good enough.

The terra-cotta artist Massimo Carbone is very intimately connected with the tradition of his craft. His apprenticeship lasted for ten years with the great Maestro Mario Mariani, who describes himself as "the last Etruscan."

In Carbone's workshop, the artist applies the techniques of the ancient world virtually unchanged. The amphorae are generally made manually and not on the turntable. Work is carried out according to the Colombino production method: the potter builds the vessel like a spiral with rolls of clay, or *lucignoli*, stacked one on top of another. Only the hands of the artist and the earthen clay go into the creation – no tools or modern technologies are used in the process.

When the clay vase or other object is dry, it is placed in an oven that is heated up to 1830 degrees Fahrenheit. Depending on the size of the piece, the firing process can last up to five days.

According to an idea given to him by the terra-cotta artist Tullio Del Bravo, Carbone now manufactures amphorae that feature rather simple decorations that are similar in form to a still life.

You can see a particularly magnificent specimen by Massimo Carbone in the Palazzo Medici Riccardi in Florence (Via Camillo Cavour 3).

Address Massimo Carbone Terrecotte, Via di Cappello 45, 50023 Impruneta |
Getting there Take the SS Firenze/Siena to the Firenze exit and follow the sign for
Tavarnuzze/Greve. After I Falciani, take a left on Via di Cappello, and it will be on the
right-hand side. | Tip The creator of the designs for the amphora featuring the pinecones
runs a restaurant in the area called Il Battibecco, which is decorated with his own
handmade terra-cotta (Viale Vittorio Veneto 38, Tel +39/055/231382, closed Sunday
evenings and Mondays).

74__The Grape Harvest Festival

Carnival in Chianti

Who won this year's parade of the wine festival? This question always grabs the headlines in the local press. What may look like a colorful Mardi Gras carnival requires a lot of preparation and hard work from those competing for the honor of "best float"; in short, it's serious business. The inhabitants of the four districts (*rioni* in Italian) in Impruneta – Sante Marie, Fornaci, Sant'Antonio, and Pallò – have taken part in this tough contest since the year 1932.

Competitors work for months on the floats and costumes for the parade, which are judged by an official jury consisting of five members selected by a notary. Each year, the costumes are designed around a different theme, but one that's always inspired by wine.

All members of the four *rioni* are volunteers and are busy planning and preparing for almost the entire year. Since 1926, the wine festival, officially known as the Festival of the Grape, has been held on the last Sunday in September. In the month leading up to the event, craftsmen work almost every night into the wee hours, tinkering with the huge floats – some nearly 30 feet high – and sewing the hundreds of costumes. Even while toiling, though, everyone's celebrating just a little. The theme-inspired floats, which are also pulled through the surrounding hills, are accompanied by marching bands and dance groups performing choreographed routines.

The winning float is chosen in the Piazza Buondelmonti, and tears of joy as well as despair are sure to flow.

The festival also includes a five-day program featuring concerts and stalls selling artisanal handicrafts and gastronomical delicacies – and a lot of Chianti. At the close of the festival, everyone celebrates with music and dancing.

Address Piazza Buondelmonti, 50023 Impruneta, www.lafestadelluva.it | **Getting there** About six miles from Florence on the A 1, exit Impruneta. | **Tip** Among the food stalls, you can try the delicious *peposo*, a peppery goulash that's a specialty of the area.

75__Villa Caruso
The love of the "greatest tenor of all time"

The 16th-century villa is located on the hills of Ponte a Signa, and the view is fantastic: To the east, the villa overlooks the town and the lake, and to the west, the rolling hills of Tuscany. A famous structure stands right in the middle of this lovely scene: the Villa Artimino of the Medici, which is known for the 100 chimneys atop its roofs.

It is clear why the Villa Caruso is also known as the Villa di Bellosguardo, because the view is really quite amazing. And almost as lovely is a walk on the terraces through the Italian gardens with their lemon and olive trees and flowers.

Originally the property was owned by the noble Pucci family, but in 1585, the abbot Alessandro, a great cultural enthusiast, turned the villa and garden into a paradisiacal retreat for his religious meditations. A great collector and promoter of young artists, he commissioned the antiquarian Giovanni Antonio Dosio from Florence with the ornate design of the villa and garden, to which the town still owes its character.

The villa changed hands several times over the centuries until 1906, when the most famous figure in the world of opera at the time, Enrico Caruso, fell under the spell of the place while on a walk with his beloved Ada Giachetti. The villa remained in his possession until his death, in 1921.

The community of Lastra a Signa bought the property from Caruso's heirs in 1995, and they had the villa and garden lavishly restored in 2012. Today, the Renaissance style is reflected in the animal sculptures by Romolo del Tadda, who also designed the Boboli Gardens in Florence.

The villa is used by the community for concerts and events and is open to the public for visits. In the evenings (Tuesday through Sunday), you can enjoy the atmosphere in the Taverna Caruso. It's especially pleasant on a warm summer night.

Address Via di Bellosguardo 54, 50055 Lastra a Signa | Getting there Take the A 1 from Florence to the Firenze-Scandicci exit, then take the S.G.C. FI-PI-LI towards Pisa to the Lastra a Signa exit, then follow the signs. | Hours Mar 1–Sep 31, Wed–Sun 10am–1pm, Fri–Sun 3–6pm; the Enrico Caruso Museum is open at the same times, www.museoenricocaruso.it | Tip An enchanting walk leads through the olive groves and orchards to the medieval town of Malmantile, whose city walls are still intact.

76 __Ghiacciaia della Madonnina

An early industrial freezer

About 70 of these round, stone giants were in operation for more than two centuries. From the end of the 17th century until the 1930s, they served as icehouses that supplied the major cities of Florence and Modena.

Between 1766 and 1779, the *strada regia modenese* was built at the behest of the Grand Duke Leopold of Tuscany. It connected Florence via Pistoia with the principality of Modena, and thereby with the Habsburg Empire, to which the grand duke belonged. During that time, the region experienced an economic boom, and the increase in the processing of iron, wood, and paper went hand in hand with the construction of early industrial structures such as saw mills and ironworks.

Along this new thoroughfare, icehouses were also built amid the Pistoia mountains. The ice was produced during winter and preserved until the spring. Rivers were dammed to form an artificial lake that completely froze over in winter. The ice was then chopped with ice picks and stored in the round stone huts, which had walls that were up to nine feet thick. The cone-shaped roof was covered with leaves, which provided further insulation.

Ice was delivered from Pistoia to Florence and the other major cities in Tuscany with great success. But in 1930, the implementation of stricter hygiene codes, as well as the invention of the electric refrigerator, put an end to this traditional business.

Some of the buildings are still intact today and can be visited, and the Ghiacciaia della Madonnina, or the Glacier of the Small Madonna, is one of the finest examples. It has been completely restored and is picturesquely situated on the river; the walk through the woods is quite atmospheric, and a guided tour is very informative.

Address 51100 Le Piastre, Pistoia | Getting there Take the SS 64 for about 8.5 miles from Pistoia towards Modena, then continue on the SS 65 until Le Piastre. | Tip The eco-museum has created a themed trail, the Itinerario del Ghiaccio (Trail of Ice), and also leads tours in English (by appointment: ecomuseo@provincia.pistoia.it, Tel +39/0573/97461). Information about other thematic nature trails in the area (such as those relating to iron or wood) can be found by visiting www.provincia.pistoia.it/ecomuseo.

77 __ The Giant Cistern

Oldest working water tank in Europe

On the road that leads from the train station to the city center of Livorno, a strange building stands out on the right side of the street: atop a row of columns sits a dome sliced right through the middle. Is it a damaged church? A theater? Or perhaps a Roman temple? The building dates from the first half of the 19th century and was built by the architect Pasquale Poccianti. It is actually a giant water tank.

The mighty neoclassical structure, built in the style of Roman thermal baths, supplied water to Livorno for nearly 100 years, between 1816 and 1912. At that time, the precious resource came by way of the Colognole aqueduct, named for the town atop Monte Maggiore, which leads over 12.5 miles from the hills of Livorno through forests and dense shrubbery down into the city.

The aqueduct and its three large reservoirs were built at a time when the city was experiencing a large economic boom. Finance, arts, publishing, and culture flourished and Livorno was proudly spruced up. It was during this period that many important public buildings were constructed, the aqueduct among them.

Poccianti was a disciple of the architecture of the French Revolution. Temple-like facades can have a lasting effect on the image of modern cities, and at the same time can hide the functionality of buildings. The architects of this era were inspired by a newfound interest in the classical. Above the portico of the *cisternone* with its eight columns, a coffered half dome rises, reminiscent of that found atop the Pantheon in Rome.

The giant cistern still serves to supply Livorno with clean water, though it is no longer the city's only reservoir. It is considered the oldest functional water tank of its kind in Europe. On the inside, it measures 125 feet wide by 138 feet long, and it has a capacity of more than 353,000 cubic feet.

Address Viale Giosuè Carducci at the corner of Via del Corona Pio Alberto, 57124 Livorno | **Getting there** Bus 1 from the train station to the Via de Larderel stop | **Tip** The entire Leopoldino aqueduct, a project by the same architect, can today be explored by foot (www.associazionegaia.net; for reservations, email asscultgaia@gmail.com or call +39/3385259192).

78_Jhonny Paranza

Fresh, hot, and delicious

This oblong piazza seems to become the city's dog park in the early evenings: ladies in their housecoats deep in conversation sit on the benches, and men stand with cigarettes in one hand and the leashes of their four-legged friends in the other.

If you were to ask the locals about Jhonny Paranza, many wouldn't be able to give you much information, though his name is certainly well known.

Paranza, whose real name is Davide Baldi, built a stand in 2008 on the Piazza Mazzini, placed bar tables and benches out front, and has since sold fried fish that many consider the best in all of Livorno. In any case, it is without a doubt unrivaled in the city in terms of price and authentic atmosphere. In the beginning, Jhonny didn't even have a business license, but nonetheless simply went about frying and selling his fish. So it goes in Livorno. Since then everything has become nice and legal.

Orders are taken by the boss himself, who writes them down on slips of paper, and service proceeds in an orderly fashion. The tables are full of guests enjoying beer or a bottle of white wine while they wait. Sometimes customers bring along their own folding chairs. And that's just fine.

The fish, calamari, shrimp, and *paranza* (a fritter made with various small fish) are freshly caught and fried according to the rules of tradition. When your order is ready, Jhonny calls out your first name, a bit like at Starbucks. He then beams and gives the crowd a thumbs-up, and the customer takes their plate. The atmosphere is unique to Livorno, just like the guests. The charm of this place is in the little things; the simple pleasure of good food and the flavor of fresh fish, crisp and delicious. The music in the background is a bit nostalgic and international – sometimes Irish, sometimes American – but it always fits.

Address Piazza Mazzini, 57126 Livorno | Getting there Bus 1 from the train station to the Piazza Mazzini stop | Hours Wed–Sun 6:30–10:30pm | Tip Nearby, the Terrazza Mascagni offers a great view of the harbor and the sea.

79___L'Ostricaio

Eating on the wall

In reality, it's just a wooden shack by the sea on the road that leads south along the coast from Livorno. But its location alone makes it worth the stop.

The hut is situated along the well-traveled Viale Italia, but also sits directly on the shore with a view of the sailboat marina just to the south. When the evening sun sinks into the sea, the view from this place is like a painting.

The shack has now been turned into a restaurant called L'Ostricaio. There are only a few tables, and it is cramped – without a reservation it is nearly impossible to get a seat.

For the sunset, however, there are usually a few spots open atop the sea wall. Two oysters and a glass of white wine are the classic fare. If the crowd is large, diners must make do with plastic plates, but the oysters taste just as good, accompanied by the breeze off the ocean.

In recent years, *il muretto*, or "the little wall," has gained a cult following among the young people of Livorno. On one beautiful evening in August, the host family – the staff list has grown from one to about ten, including fathers, uncles, sons, daughters, nephews, and nieces – took a group photograph with their biggest fans. Today the framed image hangs proudly above the bar with the caption "Muretto 2013," and everyone from Grandma to the smallest baby is pictured.

Those who would prefer to experience something a bit quieter should try the menu in the restaurant. The raw bar appetizers – oysters, prawns, and mussels – are legendary, as is the fresh fish of the day and, of course, the Livornese specialty, *cacciucco*, a seafood soup made with various fish, crabs, mussels, and squid. A rare highlight is the *tagliolini ai ricci di mare*, a thin spaghetti prepared with sea urchin, which is only available in season.

Address Viale Italia 100, 57128 Livorno | Getting there Bus 1 from the train station to the
Mare Ardenza stop | Hours 12–3pm and 6–11pm, closed Mon | Tip There is an inviting
walk along the sea all the way to the wharf.

80__ The Synagogue
Alien eyes in concrete

Those who stroll to the Duomo will come upon an impressive concrete structure at the end of the Via Carioli. Many liken it to a fossilized relic straight out of the horror movie *The Fly*, because its huge blue windows look a bit like the eyes of an insect. "Unique," say some in Livorno. "Ugly," complain many others.

The design that the famous architect Andrea di Castro delivered in 1962 for the new synagogue was certainly courageous. His inspiration was the desert tent in the story of the exodus from Egypt. It was built on the same site as an earlier synagogue constructed in 1602 and later expanded, before it was destroyed during World War II. This original building had already boasted considerable square footage; the Jewish community has played a prominent role in Livorno since the times of the Medici.

In 1593, Ferdinand I from the House of the Medici adopted the *Leggi Livornine*, which afforded rights to traders, no matter what their origin. With this law, the prince wanted to quickly attract people to this strategic city on the Mediterranean for trade purposes. The laws provided impunity and debt forgiveness for at least 25 years – except in cases of murder and counterfeiting – along with further professional and political freedom, but especially religious freedom. Thus people came to Livorno "from all over Europe with knives, but also with understanding."

During this period, communities of Greeks, English, Dutch, Germans, French, Muslims, and Jews were established. Each of them founded a nazione, had their own consul, and set up their houses of worship. A kind of "new world" on this side of the ocean found its beginnings.

Livorno became an economically prosperous multicultural port over the following centuries. The imposing building at the end of Via Carioli is still one of the three largest synagogues in Italy.

Address Piazza Benamozegh, 57123 Livorno | Getting there Bus 2 from train station to the Carioli stop | Hours By request; Tel +39/3208887044, amarantaservice@tiscali.it | Tip On Via della Madonna in Livorno, you'll find the Orthodox Church of the "United Greeks."

81 Torteria Da Gagarin
The best "five and five"

Since the 1960s, Stefano Chiappa has had the nickname "Gagarin" because he allegedly looks like the Russian cosmonaut Yuri Gagarin, the first man in space to orbit the Earth. And since 1975, at his bakery, Da Gagarin, he has served the traditional *torta di ceci*: a flat, round pancake made from water, chickpea meal, and olive oil, thinly rolled and baked in a wood oven till crispy on the outside, soft on the inside. The baked treat is served warm and seasoned with a pinch of pepper.

Da Gagarin is the only bakery that still exclusively sells the *torta*. The shop is unpretentious, with a curtain made of colorful plastic strips and no sign over the door; the interior sports tiled walls, a counter, a few tables, and a wood stove.

The legend goes that during the sea battle of Meloria in the year 1284, in which the Genoese besieged Pisa, the fleet was shaken thoroughly by a storm. The entire store of provisions was soaked, including the chickpea meal, when a barrel of oil tipped over. The mixture dried in the sun and was then eaten by the starving crew of the ship. Thus, chickpea patties landed in the cookbooks of the coast.

Those who request cecina, as the *torta di ceci* is called in Pisa, rather than *torta*, as it is customarily called in Livorno, will occasionally catch a cynical comment from Stefano's wife. In Livorno, it's customary to razz those who come from the neighboring city of Pisa.

The people of Livorno will often order *cinque e cinque*, the patties on a French-style roll. After World War II, people filled their bellies with this simple sandwich. At that time, the bread and torta each cost five lire. Those who ordered a "five and five" got both, just as they do today. It tastes especially good with eggplant, and should ideally be accompanied by a glass of *spuma bionda*, a drink similar to sparkling lemonade.

Address Via del Cardinale 24, 57123 Livorno | Getting there Bus 2 from train station to the Piazza Grande stop, near the Scali Aurelia Scafi canal and the market | Hours Mon–Sat 8:30am–2pm and 4–8pm, closed Aug | Tip Right across the street is the Mercato delle Vettovaglie, which sells all the delicacies of the region.

82 La Venezia

"A simple and happy life"

Writer Curzio Malaparte (born Kurt Erich Suckert) describes life in the Livorno neighborhood of Venezia in his 1956 book, *Those Cursed Tuscans*: "If I were from Livorno, I'd want to live on a canal in Venezia. Not on one of the great squares ... but in this simple neighborhood."

Malaparte portrays the inhabitants of the port city of Livorno as the most authentic residents in Tuscany; people who offer an alternative to the arrogance of the Florentine verisimilitude. For him, Venezia is the place to experience this authenticity.

The atmospheric neighborhood, crisscrossed with canals and bridges just like its namesake, has its origins in the 17th century, when the canals were laid out and dug for the purpose of transporting goods by boat. If you stand today on one of the bridges, you'll be taken by the feeling of walking through a smaller Venice of earlier times – devoid of today's tourists and crowds and far from the hustle and bustle of the chaotic downtown life. The neighborhood is also the only district of Livorno that did not sustain any damage during World War II.

At the Scala del Refugio 10, there is a historic building that once housed an orphanage for the children of seafarers. It became a vocational school in 1750 and prepared the orphans, all boys, to be sailors. This is where the writer Malaparte is said to have stood when he came up with the line in his book.

The director Luchino Visconti was also gripped by the charm of the district. He filmed his movie *White Nights*, which was based on the novel by Fyodor Dostoyevsky, in these streets. To this day, Venezia is a place to daydream or to practice a bit of solitary meditation. And in the summer, the Effeto Venezia Festival brings some liveliness to this peaceful area, with music in the small squares and on the canal.

Address Scala del Refugio 10, 57123 Livorno | Getting there Bus 8R from the train station to the Piazza dei Domenicani stop | Tip The Ristorante Da Michele at Scali Rosciano 10 offers fish specialties of the finest quality at reasonable prices (open daily except Mon from 7pm, Sat and Sun at noon).

83__ The Boat Harbor

Sea, land, river

About six miles from Pisa sits the seaside town of Marina di Pisa. It is a very peaceful place lying at the southern end of the Arno River estuary. The waves are held back from the bathing beaches by natural stone bays, making it a popular destination for visitors in the summer months, and the patrician houses from the 19th century determine the atmosphere of the town, reminiscent of the charming mood of the 1950s.

Recently, this sleepy town built a marina with 354 boat slips. The marina offers visitors the best place to take in the unique scenery of the area: this is where the Arno – at 150 miles, the longest river in Tuscany – flows into the sea, and from this spot you can look from the harbor up into the Apuan Alps and the San Rossore nature park.

But there's another spectacle to behold here: the nets of the fishermen on the Arno. In earlier days, the fishermen used a net in the shape of a square framed by metal bars. A rope attached to the metal rods was used to raise and lower the nets. For the most part, this was done by hand, but a motor was occasionally employed. Today, however, only hobby fishermen use the old system of nets.

Back then, the fishermen stayed in colorful cottages adjacent to the nets. They were built between 1946 and 1948 by fishermen in the Arno estuary; there are only four still standing.

The nets, both past and present, catch sardines, eels, and everything else that hangs out in the mixture of fresh and salt water. Fishermen still occasionally spend the night in the cottages when the prospects are good for a rich haul. And it is not uncommon for freshly caught fish to find their way immediately into the pan, enjoyed with a bottle of wine and the sunset.

On a clear day, the view is spectacular, with the red sun sinking into the sea and the mountains in the distance.

Address Porto di Bocca d'Arno, Via della Foce, 56128 Marina di Pisa | **Getting there** From the train station in Pisa take the Viale Antonio Gramsci. At the traffic circle, take the third exit for Via Cesare Battisti. At the next traffic circle, take the second exit to stay on the same road. It will then veer slightly to the right and become Via Porta al Mare. At the next traffic circle, take the first exit onto SS 224 and follow signs for Tirrenia / Marina di Pisa. | **Tip** Fresh fish is served on the Arno with a view of the San Rossore park at the Ristorante Retone Centotrentasei (Viale d'Annunzio 136, 56122 Marina di Pisa, Tel +39/050/8667066).

84 EquiLuna Ranch

Horse heaven with a panoramic view

Surrounded by three nature parks, this magical spot lies where the borders of the regions of Emilia Romagna, Liguria, and Tuscany all meet. It's easy to admire the ridge of the Apuan Alps from here, where the Rosario River flows through the landscape and pathways lined with grapevines and apple trees are nestled in the rolling hills in all directions.

A few years back, 10 young people built a riding stable in this idyll, where the horses live strictly according to best practices of animal welfare. The horses are allowed to form herds in the way that suits their natural social behavior. The idea of a "paddock paradise" has become a reality here. This concept was developed by a former blacksmith who had observed wild horses in Nevada for many years. He followed them in their wanderings and was fascinated by their lives, not to mention the health of their hooves, and determined it was best for domestic horses to live as similarly to their wild brethren as possible.

On the "track," as the path on which the horses move freely is known, there are as many different types of soil as possible. These may include sand, gravel, and even crushed stone. The largest incentive for the animals to move around is created through widely spaced feeding stations. Small haystacks are distributed along the entire track, making for a bucolic picture.

Even the riding lessons available are based on the principles of proximity and relationship building, not command and subordination. The offerings range from beginners' courses and trips into the mountains to specialized courses.

A ride over the trails along the river under a full moon is especially romantic. For those who prefer to keep both feet on the ground, an atmospheric walk can be just as good for enjoying the impressive mountain views.

Address EquiLuna ASD, Loc. "La Praduscella" 1, 54013 Moncigoli Fivizzano | **Getting there** From Carrara, take the A15 to the Aulla exit, then take the SS63 in the direction of Fivizzano to Valico del Cerreto; after about five miles, at the intersection head toward Slier; then about 500 yards before the bridge, take a left toward Moncigoli. After about a mile, turn right at the sign for Moncigoli; then follow signs toward the Agriturismo Praduscella. | **Tip** Right next door, at the Agriturismo Praduscella (www.agriturismolapraduscella.it), they serve specialties from Lunigiana, like *testaroli* (durum wheat crepes) with pesto.

85 Teatro dei Rassicurati
La Scala in miniature

You have to leave your car in the parking lot outside the village. From there a pathway leads you into the medieval town, with its fortress lying high atop a hill. Once there, you are rewarded with a fantastic panoramic view that stretches from the Pescia valley over Montecatini and the Pisan Mountains to Lucca.

The castle is the most visited historic building in Montecarlo, but the real treat is the town's tiny theater, the second smallest in Italy. In 1702, a group of wealthy citizens founded the Accademia degli Assicurati, or Academy of the Insured, with the aim of supporting a theater group. In the beginning, the troupe performed on a field near the city gate. When it rained, a wine cellar offered shelter.

In 1750, the Accademia acquired a building to house the performances, but in 1791, the theater was officially closed. Then in 1795, the troupe was revived.

After its reestablishment, the company was renamed Rassicurati, or the Reinsured. The Florentine architect Antonio Capretti was entrusted with designing the theater. The oval hall can accommodate 200 spectators, and is surrounded by two balconies and four lodges. The interior is reminiscent of an opera theater from the 18th or 19th century, with particularly delicate paintings.

Montecarlo has enjoyed some very special performances thanks to its theater: works by Giacomo Rossini and Giuseppe Verdi are among those that have been staged here. In 1968, the theater was slated to be demolished due to disrepair, but after protests it was restored and has since gained a cult following. Princess Grace of Monaco is said to have been one of its supporters.

Today, an amateur troupe generally puts on mostly unknown plays, but the 40-year anniversary celebration in 2013 saw the performance of works by Puccini, *The Marriage of Figaro* by Mozart, and Verdi's *Rigoletto*.

Address Teatro dei Rassicurati, Via Carmignani 14, 55015 Montecarlo | Getting there From Lucca, take the E76 toward Montechatini/Firenze for about 12.5 miles to the Capannori exit, then take the SP3 and SP31 and follow signs for Montecarlo. | Hours Through the tourist office (Via Roma 56, Mon–Sat 8am–1pm) anyone interested in touring the theater can ask to be accompanied by an employee. | Tip Be sure to try the white wine produced in Montecarlo.

86__ Villa Varramista
The home of the Piaggio family

When the iron gates are opened and visitors are allowed to enter, the stately avenue appears romantically endless; dreamy farmhouses stand here and there, and a stream flows peacefully nearby. It is idyllic perfection. "In the past, when old Piaggio was still alive, we children were allowed to play in the garden of the villa, and high above was a huge lake; today his heirs would rather maintain their privacy," recalls a pensioner who grew up here.

Visitors are welcomed only into the parlor of the villa of the Piaggio family, the inventors of the popular Vespa scooter. In the 1950s, Enrico Piaggio bought the estate, which was the seat of the famous Florentine Capponi family in the Middle Ages. The villa was the gathering place for the family and their famous friends, and frequently found its way into the tabloids.

Then, in June 1959, the wedding of the century was held at Varramista: Umberto Agnelli and Antonella Bechi Piaggio recited their vows. Giovanni Alberto, son of Antonella and Umberto, grew up in the villa and rang in his 18th birthday with a glamorous celebration. He became president of Piaggio and commuted every morning in the saddle of his Vespa to nearby Pontedera, the site of production for the cult-status scooter.

Starting in 1968, Umberto Agnelli headed the Fiat Group's international operations, and after the death of his brother, he assumed the presidency at Fiat.

In 1990, Giovanni Alberto began to cultivate exquisite red Syrah grapes on the property, and today 50,000 bottles are produced at Varramista. Following Agnelli's death in 2004, the estate was opened to the public. Tours through the vineyards and wine cellars include a tasting, and you can also book a viewing of the "salons with the Vespa." Or you can just take a fabulous walk along the avenue to the villa.

Address Fattoria Varramista, Via Ricavo Varramista, 56020 Montopoli in Val d'Arno, www.varramista.it | Getting there Take the SS Florence-Pisa-Livorno (FI-PI-LI) to the Montopoli exit, and in Valdarno drive completely around the roundabout, then turn right; before you actually enter back onto the SS FI-PI-LI, you will see the gray iron gates and a sign on the wall reading Varramista. | Hours Park: May–Sep 9am–6pm, otherwise 10am–4pm | Tip You can visit the Piaggio Museum in nearby Pontedera (www.museopiaggio.it).

87 _ Tiziano Terzani's Village

Where the tree has eyes

The road winds in tight curves from Pistoia up into the Apennines. Beyond Orsigna, you'd expect to find the end of the world. At one time, more than a thousand people lived in the village and cultivated cheese and chestnuts. Today, Orsigna and its nearly 100 inhabitants would rarely make the headlines. But as the birthplace and the last refuge of world traveler Tiziano Terzani, Orsigna spent a short time in the public eye when the film version of his last work, *The End is My Beginning*, was released in 2011, starring Bruno Ganz in the title role.

The last days of Terzani's life, recorded by his son Falco, had already garnered a cult following when they were published as a book with the same title. The writer, who was the China correspondent for the German weekly *Der Spiegel*, returned to his hometown in 2004 after being diagnosed with stomach cancer. "I feel, as my life escapes me, that it does not escape, because it is part of the life of all these trees, of life itself."

Terzani spent his final days in a *gompa*, a small Tibetan prayer hut painted red adjacent to his house where he had retired to meditate. The red house can be seen from the parking lot in Orsigna.

Hiking trail number five (CAI) takes about 30 minutes across the Case Cucciani settlement and through the forest up to the house and continues on to a venerable old chestnut tree. Terzani secured two plastic eyes he got in India to the trunk: "I did it for my grandson. Now the tree has a face. Just like a person. I want him to grasp that everything around him lives. Even this tree."

Visitors frequently leave little mementos on the tree, attaching colorful scarves and other small items, then linger a while in its shade.

The urn containing the ashes of Tiziano Terzani is buried beneath the branches.

Address Case Cucciani, 51100 Orsigna | Getting there From Pistoia, take the SS 64 to Pontepetri, then take the SS 632 for about two miles. After the village center of Pracchia, take a left and follow signs to Orsigna. | Tip Il Mulino da Berto at Via di Paoluccio 1 serves delicious treats from the Pistoia mountains in a renovated mill, including pasta made with chestnut flour and wild boar (open for lunch Sat and Sun or by reservation, Tel +39/0573/490101).

88__Cantine Basile
Wine of the sea

When you take your first sip, close your eyes and wait until the wine reaches all the taste buds in your mouth. You'll find that the flavor is strangely a bit salty. Somehow, the wine here tastes of the ocean. Indeed, the slopes on which the grape vines of the Vermentino bianco or the Sangiovese grow reach almost all the way down to the beaches of Versilia.

This seaside area has been famous since the 1950s mostly for its rollicking nightlife, especially in Viareggio. Less well known, but still interesting for wine lovers, are the area's vineyards, less than 10 miles north of the party zone, near the town of Pietrasanta, which is renowned for its artists. The heavy Chianti, the noble Brunello, and the well-rounded red from Maremma all enjoy a good reputation in Tuscany, but the fresh, fruity Vermentino bianco and substantial Vermentino nero, which really only thrive here in Versilia, are typically underestimated. As is the elegant rosé made from Syrah, Merlot, and Vermentino grapes.

For more than 50 years, the Basile family has cultivated grapevines in this region under the historic moniker Capitanato di Pietrasanta. It is rumored that as far back as the times of the Medici rule, even Michelangelo happily enjoyed a carafe of their wine. The area here is tiny in comparison to the other growing regions in Tuscany, but the terrain is unique thanks to the nature and composition of the soil. The influences on the soil range from the marble in the Apuan Alps, which makes the earth rich in calcium, to the extreme proximity to the sea, which gives the air a high iodine content. The wine matures sheltered from the wind and under the sun, which shines here in full force.

At the Cantine Basile, you can taste the different varieties of wine and learn the details of viticulture by the sea from the owners. The tour includes a visit to the vineyards.

Address Via Provinciale per Vallecchia 260, 55044 Pietrasanta | Getting there Take the highway A 11 Firenze/Mare to the Versilia exit, then head toward Pietrasanta, about a mile outside of the town center. | Hours By appointment, contact cantinebasile@gmail.com | Tip The Il Posto restaurant in Pietrasanta, at Piazza Carducci 12, serves Capitanato di Pietrasanta wines (www.ristoranteilposto.it).

89 __ The Labyrinthine Streets
Getting lost in Pisa

If you try to ask someone in the old town of Pisa for help in finding the Via della Croce Rossa or the Via del Porton Rosso, don't be surprised if a helpful response or any useful information is hard to come by, even from a third-generation Pisan, and even if you are standing only one block away at the time. "Never heard of it, certainly not here." The roads do exist, but you'll search in vain for any signs.

Very few people actually know the names of these winding streets, whose design dates back to Pisa's turbulent past as a naval power. In some corners of the city, especially near the Arno River, which runs through Pisa and then later flows into the sea, the narrow and sloping streets awaken a sense of the city's past. The Ottomans drew the city map here: not a single street is straight; every street ends diagonally to the next.

It was all part of the defensive strategy on the Mediterranean – to spread out the independent cities to impede penetration by an enemy. Atop the tall tower houses, the skyscrapers of their time, the people of Pisa could spy invaders from afar. If their opponents managed to approach the city, they would be thwarted by the tangle of narrow, dark alleys. Just like in a maze, each street turns in the exact opposite direction at every corner, making progress akin to running in a zigzag. In this way, the disoriented enemies were often forced to surrender or retreat.

Some houses in this part of the city along the Arno are among the oldest buildings in Pisa, and walls dating back to the year 900 have been discovered. In these romantic and simultaneously somewhat menacing streets, Pisa's most traditional cinema, the Cinema Lumière, has stood at Vicolo del Tidi 6 since 1905. It was recently reopened following an extensive renovation, and also features a bar and live music.

Address Via della Croce Rossa, Via del Porton Rosso, 56126 Pisa | Getting there The labyrinthine alleys are behind the Lungarno Pacinotti and the Palazzo Agostini. From the train station take bus Lam Rosso or 4 to the Pacinotti 3 stop. | Tip The small Osteria La Mescita at Via Domenico Cavalca 2 serves refined dishes like cod with peppers, raisins, and pine nuts and a nice selection of wines from small but high-quality wineries.

90__Santo Stefano dei Cavalieri

Battle flags in the house of God

In the 16th century, pirates plagued every coast of the Tuscan archipelago, as well as the islands nearby. Attacks by not only Saracens, but also by English, French, and Spanish corsairs were a part of everyday life. Today, defiant fortresses testify to the defensive needs of the time, but the Medici had a special force at their disposal to fend off these attacks.

The Cavalieri di Santo Stefano were a military order founded in 1562 by Cosimo I. Under the protection of the Pope, they were allowed to establish their own fleet with which they fought against the pirates who roamed the Mediterranean Sea. The spoils of the Cavalieri undermined the status of the knights as defenders of the Catholic faith, but the flags they took in victory were objects of prestige, both for them and for their clients, the Pope and the Medici. After a battle was won, the flags that had been confiscated from the enemy were paraded through the streets in celebratory marches, and were then displayed with honor on the walls of the church.

Thus trophies from the naval battles – among them the famous Battle of Lepanto – decorate the nave of the church of Santo Stefano in Pisa. More than 90 flags are preserved. A portion of the collection is framed in glass; the heavier, better-preserved flags hang between the high windows. The flags of silk or cotton depict symbolic motifs, such as crescents, the sword of the Prophet Mohammed with two blades, a scimitar, stars, Fatima's hand, or chevron stripes.

But the knights of Santo Stefano captured a much larger number of flags than are exhibited here. This is evidenced in the *Libro delle prede delle bandiere e degli schiavi*, or the "Book of the booty of flags and slaves."

Address Piazza dei Cavalieri, 56126 Pisa | **Getting there** Piazza dei Cavalieri is in the city center. Take bus 4 from the train station to the Maria 1 stop. | **Tip** Just a five-minute walk in the direction of the Arno is the Piazza delle Vettovaglie, with its picturesque marketplace and small restaurants.

91 Agriturismo Le Dogane

Where the wild torrent rushes

The road that leads to the Agriturismo Le Dogane winds through a magical forest of chestnut trees, past abandoned mills, and down to the River Lima. As you get closer to the riverbed, don't be surprised to see a baby goat or two napping in the middle of the road. After all, this is a farm.

At the end of the lane on the right-hand side, you'll come upon a structure that looks straight out of the Middle Ages, protected somehow from the ravages of time: the Castruccio bridge, with its simple archway, spans the Lima, which flows down from the slopes of the Libro Aperto.

The stone structure, a prime example of an historic mule track bridge, was erected in 1317 on orders of the mercenary leader Castruccio Castracani from Lucca, who fought with the Guelphs against the Ghibellines from Pistoia. Throughout the Middle Ages, the two political groups were in combat. The basis of the conflict was the power struggle between the emperor and the Pope. At that time, the bridge was the only connection between the territories of Pistoia and Lucca.

Later on, tollbooths were constructed at either end of the bridge. These have been recently restored, and a young couple has established a small bed and breakfast affiliated with the farm next door. The bridge is visible from every room in the small accommodation, whose walls date back to the 14th century.

The interior of the *agriturismo* features original medieval stone walls, terra-cotta floors, and wood-beamed ceilings. In the restaurant, which is open daily, you can sample specialties from Tuscany. Or perhaps you'd prefer one of the freshly caught brown trout plucked from the raging river.

Be sure to linger awhile alongside the river after your meal and listen to the water as it rushes beneath the historic bridge.

Address Loc. Lambure 1, 51020 Piteglio, www.agriturismoledogane.it | **Getting there** From Pistoia, take the SS 66 "dell'Abetone e del Brennero" (Brenner state road) to the village of Piastre, then take a left toward Piteglio and follow the signs for Ponte di Castruccio until you reach the river. | **Tip** A wildly romantic route along the old paths of penitential processions starts at the church of Santa Maria Assunta, built in 1271 in Popiglio, and leads to the Castruccio bridge.

92__The Tower Houses
Three-room apartments from the 14th century

The town of Filattiera stretches between the mountains and hills, along the path of the Magra River up to the foothills of the Apennines. The village of 2,000 residents in the province of Lunigiana in northern Tuscany was once a Byzantine fortification, but today is a rare destination for visitors.

Even more hidden is the medieval village of Ponticello – located just over a mile away – which dates back to the 14th century, making it one of the oldest villages in the province. Situated on the Via Francigena, the ancient pilgrim route, it seems as though time has stood still in this quaint enclave. Pointed and rounded arches and vaults connect the streets and buildings.

Among the outstanding original architectural elements of Ponticello are the stone tower houses. These impressive square buildings were typical fortified dwellings in the 14th century, each essentially a three-room apartment, except that the rooms are stacked one on top of another.

People had access to the building via a retractable ladder, and a trap door led into the lowest space, where food and water provisions were stocked. The ground floor had neither windows nor doors, there were only slits through which the light penetrated. Today, many of the tower houses are rented out as vacation homes.

August is the only time of the year when there's anything going on in Ponticello, with *I Mestieri nel Borgo* (Crafts in the Village), when the old techniques of medieval craftsmanship are revived. For three days leading up to the Ferragosto holiday on August 15th, you can watch artisans as they work stone, weave baskets, do woodcarving, and make bobbin lace. And of course dishes from yesteryear are served on long tables in the narrow streets from the 14th to the 17th of August. There are also regional wines to sample and plenty of festive music.

Address 54023 Ponticello di Filattiera | Getting there From Carrara, take the A 15 for approximately 31 miles to the Pontremoli exit. After the tollbooth, turn right onto the curved road and then right onto the SS 62 toward Cisa. Continue for just under two miles to Scorcetoli, and turn left at the Ristorante Pantera Rosa, then left again after the railway crossing. Continue on to Ponticello. | Tip At the Romanesque church of Santo Stefano in Sorano, about a half mile outside Ponticello, you can see two original sandstone figures of Celtic-Lunigianan origin.

93 __ Santissima Annunziata
A temple within a church

The city of Pontremoli lies 28 miles northwest of Carrara, in the valley of the Magra River in the Apuan Alps, and is dominated by the former fortress of Cacciaguerra. The few tourists who visit this town of 8,000 residents usually head straight for the Stelae Museum housed in the Castello del Piagnaro.

But only about a half a mile south, a great treasure is housed in the church of the Santissima Annunziata. The building originally dates from the 15th century. Legend has it that one day the Virgin Mary appeared to a girl who was tending a flock of sheep here. The miracle attracted many pilgrims, so Augustinian monks built a monastery with a church, which they furnished with precious works of art.

The small octagonal temple standing in the center of the spacious Gothic nave surprises many visitors today. It was built in 1526 and is decorated with works by various artists. The temple, designed by the sculptor Jacopo Sansovino along with artists affiliated with his school, is extremely complex. The dome is reminiscent of Brunelleschi's dome in Florence. Inside, the fresco, *Annunciation*, from the 15th century, is hidden behind the altar. It depicts the miraculous apparition of the angel to the Virgin Mary.

Above the altar is a work by Luca Cambiaso that portrays the adoration of the Magi flanked by two frescoes – one of Saint Ambrose and the other of Saint Jerome. In the rear portion of the temple, a marble statue of St. Augustine sits in a niche, but its artist is unknown.

And when you look further to the left into the sacristy, you will find a richly decorated room with wood inlays, all of which Brother Francesco Battaglia painstakingly created by hand in the 16th century. He is said to have taken eight years to complete this extraordinary work.

Address Santissima Annunziata, Via Nazionale, 54027 Pontremoli | Getting there
Located about 30 miles from Carrara on the A15 (Pontremoli exit). The church lies
before the village. | Hours Don Lorenzo, the parish priest, must unlock the church;
Tel +39/333/6372000 | Tip Farfalle in Cammino leads bicycle tours "through the
Middle Ages" on Sundays during the summer in this area. To make a reservation, visit
www.farfalleincammino.org.

94__The Lock at Santa Lucia

An ingenious generator for industry

Prato has been known for its wool and fabric production since the Middle Ages. Just 12.5 miles northeast of Florence, this Tuscan city is one of the few that did not suffer terribly during the recent global economic crisis. About 9,000 small and medium-sized craft enterprises still produce and export textiles in Prato, despite increased competition from Asia.

One of the foundations of this long-standing commercial success is the River Bisenzio. Or, more specifically, the construction of canals in the area, which provided optimal conditions for the production of goods. The water management system is one of the most refined and oldest in all of Italy. Artificial channels nearly 33 miles long begin at the locks in Santa Lucia and course through the entire city of Prato, including the city center. At their end, five open water routes flow into the Ombrone River.

The initial design and specifications for the canal system date as far back as the time of the Romans, who sought to control the rising waters of the area's swamps. But completion of the system dates to the technologically savvy Middle Ages. In addition to the draining of the swamps, the system also had an irrigation function, but above all the canals served as the driver for 58 water mills, whose energy output helped the industrial settlement thrive over the following centuries in paper making, metalworking, and, most important, cloth production.

Today, the canal system is part of the city's industrial history, and most of the waterways run underground. Only the lock at Santa Lucia still stands as a monument to the system's glorious past. Take a scenic bike ride for about six miles from Mezzana to Santa Lucia along the Bisenzio River for an especially pleasant experience.

Address Via Bologna 342, 59100 Prato | Getting there From Prato take Viale Galileo Galilei along the Bisenzio or by bicycle (rentals available at Obrii, Viale Galileo Galilei in Prato, Tel +39/3317805344, www.obrii.it) | Tip The textile museum (Museo del Tessuto), at Via Santa Chiara 24, documents the industrial history of Prato.

95 Museo della Deportazione

A museum of remembrance

The part of Prato known as Figline looks like a peaceful suburban residential area, where old men play cards in the back room of the Circolo L'ARCI (Associazione Ricreativa e Culturale Italiana). But it is still best known for one historic day: September 6, 1944, when 29 partisans of the Bogardo Buricchi brigade were hanged under the bridge here by a Nazi Wehrmacht unit in retreat. Thus the club's building is dedicated to the 29 victims and an eerie monument under the bridge bears witness to the massacre. Directly across from the site of the atrocity is the Museo della Deportazione (Deportation Museum).

Roberto Castellani was one of 136 partisans who lived in Prato. As a result of a general strike that brought the textile industry to a standstill, the then 17-year-old was deported to the concentration camp at Mauthausen and later to the sub-camp at Ebensee. From the whole of Tuscany there were 951 political deportees sent to the camps – 133 of whom were from Prato. Castellani is one of the few survivors and is a member of ANED, the national association of former political prisoners of the concentration camps; he is also a cofounder of the museum.

The Museo della Deportazione was inaugurated in 2002 and funded by the city of Prato, which wanted it to be a place that could contribute to the cultural and commercial development of its citizens, both young and old. It remembers the men and women who were deported and takes you on a somber journey through a Nazi concentration camp. Some of the objects on display in the *museo* are originals, while other exhibits are reproductions. The testimonials of survivors, which were recorded and are presented as videos, are particularly moving.

The museum also houses the Documentation Centre of Deportation and Resistance.

Address Via di Cantagallo 250, 59100 Prato | Getting there Take the A 11 highway (Pistoia–Florence) to the Prato Est exit and follow the signs toward Centro / Poggio a Caiano. Continue onto Viale Leonardo da Vinci, then turn right onto the Viale C. Zhou toward Vaiano to Via Cantagallo, then turn left and follow the signs for the Museo della Deportazione. | Hours Mon–Fri 9:30am–12:30pm, Mon, Thu, Sat, Sun 3–6pm (June–Sep 4–7pm) | Tip The memorial to the 29 hanging victims is opposite the museum under the bridge.

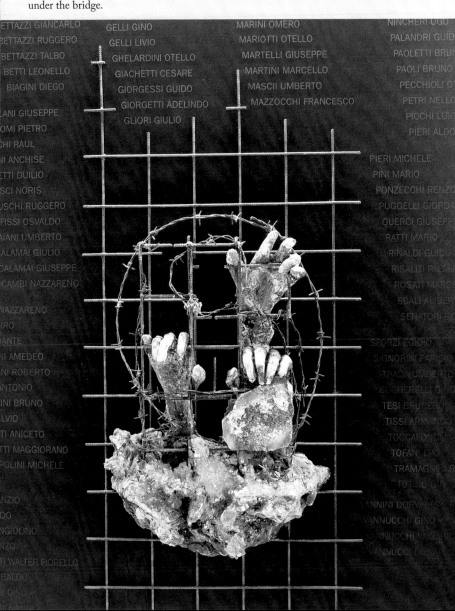

96 Monte Forato

A slap upside the head from the devil

The unusual twin peaks of Monte Forato can be seen from the terrace in front of the cathedral in Braga, or from the beach in Forte dei Marmi, where you can watch the fiery sunset behind its silhouette. At such a distance, it looks like a sleeping giant with his mouth agape. Between its peaks, the mountain is pierced with a hole.

The rock arch at an altitude of nearly 4,000 feet measures almost 100 feet across; it was created over thousands of years through wind and water erosion in the calcium-rich rock. And as with almost all wonders of nature, there is a legend that has arisen to explain its origin.

The pious San Pellegrino was resting on his way to Jerusalem atop a mountain in the valley of the Serchio, where the abbey of San Pellegrino in Alpe now stands. The devil sought endlessly to seduce him, trying to put a halt to his pilgrimage. He tried all sorts of tricks, at one point even transforming himself into a beautiful girl. Yet San Pellegrino was unwavering! Because it was the devil, who always took things too far, he turned himself into a giant monster and slapped the pious man on his ear so hard that he was sent spinning three times around. Now the pilgrim had had enough: he answered with a smack that caused the devil to fly over the Serchio Valley through the middle of the mountain, landing on the other side at the bottom of a lake. And that is how the hole in the mountain is said to have been created.

In any case, this natural work of art is fascinating. Monte Forato has its largest audience at the summer solstice party in Pruno di Stazzema, when thousands of people watch as the sun rises twice. The first time, it shines in the opening, then disappears quickly behind the rocks, only to rise for a second time on the horizon. Musical performances contribute to the festive atmosphere.

Address Piazza della Pieve di San Nicolò, 55040 Pruno di Stazzema | Getting there Take the A 11 to the Forte dei Marmi exit, then the SP 68 to Ripa-Ponterossi and continue on the SP 9 through Seravezza, Fontaneto, Via Cardoso, and Via Vallinventri. Then take a sharp left on Via Monte Forato to Pruno. | Tip Take a guided hike up Monte Ferrato. Suitable only for experienced alpine hikers – it's five and a half hours of hiking, three uphill (www.liveyourtuscany.com).

97 __ Castello di Sonnino

From the perspective of the foreign minister

Your imagination will be set into motion the moment you gaze upon this castle from the beach below: from up there, you know the view must be stunning! This was probably the same thought that Sidney Sonnino had when he chose to make his home on this site, high above the coast of Livorno.

Sonnino was one of the most important representatives of Italian liberalism. As Italy's foreign minister, it was he who signed the secret Treaty of London with the Allies in 1915: in return for entering the war on their side, Italy's territorial claims were to be guaranteed. But at the Paris peace conference after the war, all his hopes were bitterly dashed, and Sonnino withdrew from politics shortly thereafter.

While still serving as foreign minister, however, he acquired this former fortress dating from the 8th century on the Costa Azzurra, the rough and romantically rocky coast between Ardenza and Castiglioncello. Up here, in perfect silence, the sensitive soul dedicated himself to his library until his death.

About five yards below the fortress is a grotto where the monks from a monastery in the hinterland had allegedly withdrawn for meditation some time prior. It is here that the former politician decided he would like to be buried. Sonnino even built the bulky sarcophagus himself.

Looking down from the grave, you can view the horizon with its blur of azure sea. He engraved his year of birth on the stone himself, and his year of death eventually came in 1922. It is hard to imagine a better place for eternal rest.

New owners bought the castle from Sonnino's heirs in the 1980s, and made it accessible to the public shortly thereafter. Those who don't visit the castle itself can still admire it from below just as the people of Livorno do while swimming in the waters of the Cala del Leone bay, between the rocks of the cape of Romito.

Address Via del Littorale 365, 57128 Quercianella, www.quercianellasonnino.it, quercianellaproloco@gmail.com | Getting there From Livorno, head south through Ardenza in the direction of Quercianella. Just before entering the town on the coastal road, take a right onto Via del Littorale to number 365, where you'll see the sign for Castello di Sonnino. | Hours Mar–Oct, open for tours on selected dates. Visit the website, or email for availability and reservations. | Tip A half mile farther south before entering town, Via Cristophero Columbo branches off. At the end there is a footpath that leads below to the dreamy Baia del Rogiolo, with lounge chairs and a restaurant.

98__The Ancient Margheri Mill

The watermill on the rushing stream

The miller Roberto Cerbai is passionate about his work yet outraged to be part of a dying industry: there used to be 400 watermills in the Mugello, but only three are still in operation. Clearly this does not appropriately pay tribute to the historical heritage of the region.

Watermills are among the most important technical achievements of mankind – their invention replaced muscle power with the natural energy of water. Margheri Mill is probably the earliest surviving example in Tuscany. The stone watermill is the jewel of the hilly green landscape north of Florence, where all four of the rivers that flow northward spring forth. It was built in the year 845 and works perfectly to this day.

Cerbai grinds chestnuts and corn in the mill, and the high season runs from the first Sunday in October until Christmas. As he oversees the mechanical marvel every day from 9:30am until evening, he knows the machine's inner workings like no other. His family owns the house and the mill. The property sits romantically on a rushing stream. Roberto cares for the mechanics of the mill himself, even manufacturing his own replacement parts, since naturally, there are no longer any on the market.

How much work the mill can produce is dependent upon the season and the velocity and volume of the stream, since the water drives the mill. But the location, known as Madonna dei Tre Fiumi, or Our Lady of the Three Rivers, signifies that the three waterways that meet here usually provide the mill with abundant water.

Understandably, only small amounts of flour are produced at the mill, but it is of the highest quality. In any case, you must try the chestnut-flour tortelli typical of Margheri, or bring home some flour to make your own polenta or tortellini.

Address Madonna dei Tre Fiumi 18, 50032 Ronta | Getting there From Florence, take
the road to Borgo San Lorenzo for about 25 miles and then take the SP 55 toward
Faenza. Follow the signs to Ronta. | Tip You can try the famous *tortelli rontesi* at the
restaurant / hotel I Tre Fiumi directly across from the mill.

99__White-Sand Beaches
Caribbean flair … with carbonate

The turquoise sea sparkles as far as the eye can see. On the dazzling white-sand beach, children build castles while teenagers splash in the water. A stand offers brightly colored bikinis and ice-cream bars at reasonable prices. Everyone has that summertime glow. A beach like this with a Caribbean flair does not exist anywhere else in Italy, and its residents are very proud. The parking lot is huge and the crowds are enormous, especially in August.

But the *spiagge bianche*, or white beaches, as they are known to the locals, are the greatest paradox of beach-going on the Italian coast. The origin of the fantastic colors cannot be explained by geology or nature; they are caused by additives to the sand and seawater.

The answer to the riddle is found by turning your gaze from the sea to the land. There you'll see rising up from the landscape the cooling towers, chimneys, and halls of the Belgian company Solvay SA, which has produced chemicals here since 1941. Solvay is among the 10 largest chemical manufacturers in the world, known for sodium carbonate, chlorine, caustic soda, polyvinyl chloride, and polyethylene.

Until 2010, about 500 tons of mercury were discharged into this water, and sodium carbonate and calcium carbonate continue to flow. The calcium carbonate acts as the "white giant," bleaching the sand snow-white and turning the seawater a delicate, tropical-looking turquoise.

There are warning signs posted that prohibit swimming, though they are frequently defaced almost immediately.

Commercials are often filmed on these white beaches, and the region's Association of Hoteliers fight for the title of the "most beautiful beach in Italy," and have even sought to change the area's name from Rosignano Solvay to Marina di Rosignano, to keep the Caribbean image intact.

Address Via Gigli, 57016 Rosignano Solvay | **Getting there** From Livorno, take the Aurelia southbound to the Rosignano Marittimo exit and continue toward Rosignano Solvay/Castillioncello. Pass straight through the roundabout, then turn right on Via Lungomonte. Take a right on Via Cava, and in the next roundabout, take the second exit for Via Campigny Sur Marne. Continue on the Via Cavallereggi, and at the next roundabout, take Via Vittorio Veneto. At the next roundabout, take a right onto Via Gigli to the parking lot. It's tricky to find, so if in doubt, ask for directions to the *spiagge bianche*. | Tip *Cacciucco*, a soup made with various types of fish, crab, mussels, and squid, is served at the Garage Café on Via Caduti di Nasiriya in the industrial area of Rosignano Marittimo (12–3pm and 8–11pm except Sun).

100__ The Crazy Cart

1,400 "fiaschi" and not one fiasco

Pulled by two Chianina bulls, the wagon known as the *carro matto*, or the "crazy cart," was once the means by which Chianti wine was transported from Pontasieve to Florence. 1,400 bottles of Chianti were artfully packed in a work of millimetric precision on the cart, which first made the 12.5-mile journey in 1788.

Chianti has been cultivated on the slopes of the Arno and the Sieve valleys since the 15th century. Historically, when the cart arrived in Florence after its adventurous voyage, the harvest was celebrated with a festive parade featuring the *caro matto* that ended at the Piazza della Signoria. Beforehand, the bottles were blessed by church dignitaries, and afterward, even the common people came out to partake.

The Chianti was stored in *fiaschi* (singular *fiasco*), the bulbous straw-covered bottles that originated in the late Middle Ages when guidelines were laid down for the volume of wine bottles – 2.28 liters. A layer of oil was poured on top of the wine inside each bottle as protection against oxidation. The *fiasco*, however, could withstand the pressure of the cork. A lead seal on the straw wrapping would prevent abuse, and the straw jacket was designed to protect the glass, which, to date, is still handblown and correspondingly fragile.

In the 1970s, when quantity became prized over quality, the rounded bottle became less desirable. And in 1986, in the wake of the methanol scandal, the reputation of the Rufina region's wines collapsed. The Chianti Rufina ultimately regained its good name, however, and its fiaschi are mostly collected now as souvenirs.

An example of the crazy cart can be viewed in the wine museum in the Villa di Poggio Reale in Rufina. Every year, during the last week of September, Rufina celebrates the grape harvest, and the cart sets off on its symbolic journey into Florence on Saturday afternoon.

Address Villa Poggio Reale, Viale Duca della Vittoria 7, 50068 Rufina | **Getting there** From Florence, through Bagno a Ripoli and then the SS 67 via Pontasieve to Rufina. | **Hours** Wed, Fri 3–7pm, Sat 9am–1pm and 3–6pm, Sun 10am–1pm; guided tours available by appointment, contact winelabrufina@gmail.com | **Tip** If you'd like to sample the Chianti Rufina out of season, the Colognole winery at Via del Palagio 15 in Colognole Rufina organizes tastings (www.colognole.it; for reservations, email reception@colognole.it).

101__ Villa Montepaldi
The science of wine

The Villa Montepaldi's location in the hills of Florence in the heart of the Chianti region is just one of the reasons why it's worthwhile to trace the wine culture of Tuscany here. A second is the property itself, which is surprising in its history and details. The villa was originally owned by the Accioli, a wealthy banking and merchant family, who were forced to hand it over to Lorenzo I de' Medici in 1487 to pay a debt. Today, the property is a classic example of Medici villa architecture.

In 1627, the Corsini family from Florence bought the property and built a thriving farm, where they cultivated grains, vineyards, and olive groves. In later years, Marc Chagall was among those who tasted the noble vintages, and artists have always been counted among friends of the family.

Since the University of Florence acquired the farm in 1989, they have operated an innovative research center with modern equipment on a nearly 780-acre site adjacent to the regular wine production area. There you can find scientists experimenting with the method for making champagne, or tinkering with the cultivation of various types of grain – as it was done during the Middle Ages – in order to make them resistant to parasitic infections, and also to taste better.

The grapevines, which are grown on 111 acres, to a large extent consist of the full-bodied Sangiovese grape. In earlier times, wine was consumed mainly to provide the body with energy rather than for the purpose of intoxication. At least that's what the Dottore will tell you on one of the tours he leads for visitors upon request. His authoritative free tour of the production rooms, wine cellar, and the villa can be counted as the third reason to visit here. A taste of the Sangiovese or the Vin Santo, the dessert wine from Tuscany that is aged in wooden barrels, rounds off the visit.

Address Via Montepaldi 12, 50026 San Casciano Val di Pesa, www.villamontepaldi.it, commerciale@villamontepaldi.it | Getting there From Florence, take the A1 to the Firenze-Impruneta exit, then the SS toward Siena to the first exit for San Casciano Val di Pesa. After a couple of miles, before the entrance to the village of San Casciano, you will reach the roundabout for Empoli-Cerbaia; take the second exit. After a few miles, turn left at the sign for Montepaldi and follow the cypress-lined avenue up to the Villa Montepaldi. | Hours By appointment only; email commerciale@villamontepaldi.it | Tip You can buy wine, pasta, and olive oil at the small shop next to the villa.

102__The Cerratelli Collection

The tailor's old clothes

In the 1964 film *Circus World*, actress Rita Hayworth wore a stunning emerald-green evening gown decked out with precious stones that made the star – 46 years old at the time – look incredibly sexy. This is just one of the jewels in the collection of the Foundation Cerratelli, put on exhibit to celebrate the 100th anniversary of the Casa d'Arte Cerratelli in Florence. The foundation has inherited a large part of the company's collection of historical costumes and has at least one exhibition each year in the rooms of the beautiful historic Villa Roncione.

A total of approximately 300,000 costumes, dating from the Middle Ages through the early 19th century, in the fields of cinema, theater, opera, and ballet, are a veritable treasure trove for the foundation, which also owns nearly 20,000 old film posters.

At each exhibition a different theme is celebrated, and about 40 costumes find their way back into the spotlight. They are as varied as the renowned costume designer's customers – from opera producers to directors of spaghetti Westerns and film auteurs.

The Casa d'Arte Cerratelli was founded in 1919 by Arturo Cerratelli, an opera singer who collected stage costumes. From the 1930s, the production of films at the Cine Città studios in Rome provided significant business for the company, and soon the costume makers had an excellent reputation internationally.

Some of the famous films they outfitted were *El Cid*, *The Fall of the Roman Empire*, and *The Taming of the Shrew*. Later, they worked on the British feature *A Room with a View* (1985). The Metropolitan Opera in New York, the Chicago Opera Theater, Covent Garden in London, and La Scala in Milan have all also ordered historical costumes from Casa d'Arte Cerratelli for their performances.

Address Villa Roncioni, Via Statale dell'Abetone 226, Pungnano, 56017 San Giuliano Terme, www.fondazionecerratelli.it | Getting there About 7.5 miles from Pisa to Pugnano on the SS 12 (Via del Brennero). | Hours For exhibition dates/times, visit the Foundation Cerratelli's website | Tip Concerts featuring Puccini's music take place on Sundays in the beautiful garden of the historic Villa Borbone at Viale dei Tigli 50 in Viareggio, about 12.5 miles away (www.villaborbone.net).

103_ The Pedestrian Suspension Bridge

An adrenaline rush 130 feet in the air

From this point of view, the Pistoia mountains look like a jungle. The forest is penetrated by an ingenious steel construction with a length of over 720 feet: one of the longest pedestrian suspension bridges in the world connects the two banks of the Lima River.

Before stepping onto the bridge, you'll need to prepare with a few deep breaths, because the walk across can entail a major adrenaline rush. Every movement you make will cause the metal wires to swing all the way to the other side.

However exciting the crossing, the original purpose of the bridge was not for fun but a practical one: it guaranteed workers from the village of Popiglio a shorter route to their jobs on the other side of the river.

Before its construction, workers had to travel nearly four miles each day by foot between work and home. In the 1920s, the steel-works of Campo Tizzoro, the Società Metallurgica Italiana (now called Europa Metalli), was located on the other side of the river in Mammiano. It's hard to imagine that in this idyllic green locale, bustling industrial plants once dominated the landscape.

Vincenzo Scotti Douglas, an engineer and director of the steel mills at that time, issued the order to build the bridge. Steel cables were anchored with chains into concrete blocks to bear the load for the structure. A massive iron frame with metal bars forms the roughly three-foot-wide catwalk. Construction took about two years, and about 30 workers were employed in the undertaking. The incredible feat of engineering has even found admiration from experts abroad.

The bridge was restored in 2004, and is completely safe. Since 2014, it has also been lit at night, for even more of a thrill.

Address Loc. Mammiano Basso, 51028 San Marcello Pistoiese | Getting there From Pistoia, take the SS 66 "dell'Abetone e del Brennero" (Brenner State Road) to San Marcello Pistoiese. From there, head toward Piteglio on the SS 66 for about four miles, then follow the signs for Ponte Sospeso up to a bar with a terrace. The last portion feels a little adventurous. | Tip On weekends, families often visit the small artificial lake with its restaurant and picnic area.

104_ The Pig Butcher
Pigging out in Garfagnana

In addition to the sales counter, Cesare Casci has a second counter in his butcher shop covered with colorful little pigs from France, Germany, Holland, and other parts of Europe. His friends bring him back these souvenirs from their travels, because Cesare is, so to speak, the expert in Garfagnana when it comes to pigs.

Thirty-five years ago, his father brought to life the Sagra del Maiale, a popular annual folk festival in August where pigs and pork play the central role. Cutlets of porchetta (the grilled Tuscan suckling pig served on a roll) are cooked atop huge grills, as are pig livers known as *fegatelli di maiale*, a traditional favorite in the region. You can also try the salty bread cakes prepared by the women of the village.

For everyone, though, the highlight of the festival is the couples' dance and the raffle. The prize is a no-brainer: a pig weighing 220 pounds and other delicacies from the house of Cesare Casci.

There are *sagre* – festivals with a culinary theme – everywhere in Tuscany, but in the province of Garfagnana (a mountainous area north of Lucca known for its natural beauty) their frequency is remarkable. From April to November, you'll find up to 10 festivals a month: the festival of chestnut flour, where you'll find delicious pasta dishes; the festival of *minestella*, where you can try just about any variety of vegetable soup imaginable; the festival of the *raviolo*, which celebrates the famous stuffed pasta; even the festival of the wild boar.

Cesare Casci's pigs live on his farm, alongside goats, chickens, a calf, and a peacock. You can visit and sample some ham in the garden or parlor, or perhaps a schnitzel or sausage, or even *cotechini con fagioli*, a very spicy Italian sausage made from the neck, head, and rind of the pig and served with hearty beans – a substantial dish. A nap in the garden is a nice way to digest.

Address Loc. Arsenale, 55051 San Pietro in Campo | Getting there From Barga, head toward Castelnuovo Garfaniana, keep right after Mologno to the sign for Arsenale, and after about 300 feet, turn left at the curve onto the small road. At the end of the street you'll find Cesare il Macellaio. | Tip The house and museum of the Italian poet Giovanni Pascoli is about two miles away (Casa Museo, Via Caprona 4, Castelvecchio Pascoli, www.casapascoli.it).

105 __ Fortezza delle Verrucole
A fishy fortress

The fortress known as Fortezza delle Verrucole is one of the most important military installations in the province of Garfagnana, but it is rarely visited. The most extraordinary thing about it is its long and narrow wall. Constructed directly on the rocky ground without a foundation, the wall's shape is adapted to the profile of the hill. In addition, the plan view of the fortress – from a bird's-eye perspective – reveals that the whole thing is built in the shape of a fish.

The path up is a bit difficult. Once you finally reach the top, however, you're rewarded with an incredible view. The road winds upward several hundred feet to the village of San Romano in the Apuan Alps. At the end, there is a long stone-paved walkway that leads up to the fort.

The history of the fort began more than 1,000 years ago, with the Gherardinghi family. They formed an alliance with Pisa to defend themselves against the territorial claims of Lucca in Garfagnana. But in 1170, the Lucchese prevailed, and the Gherardinghi lost power and influence. Over the following centuries, the fortress was often a bone of contention between rival parties in Tuscany. In the course of the 18th century – with the invasion of the French – the province of Garfagnana was again placed under the rule of Lucca and the fort was abandoned and left to rot, like many other once-magnificent medieval sites.

In the 1990s, the municipality of San Romano purchased the site from a private citizen and had it fully restored. Since 2012, it has been presented as a "jewel among military structures," according to the experts. A tour demonstrates life in the fortress during the 13th century.

On the terrace, then as now, you'll find the perfect spot for observation – and thus the beautiful view of the mountain ridge of the Apuan Alps, Emilia Romagna, and Tuscany.

Address Via Roma 9, 55038 San Romano di Garfagnana, www.fortezzaverrucolearcheopark.it | Getting there From Castelnuovo di Garfagnana, pass through Pontecosi and Sillicagnana to San Romano (about seven miles on a curvy road). Continue through the village, then follow signs for Verrucole. | Hours Fri–Sun 10am–7pm, in the summer to 9pm | Tip It's worth seeing the Rocca Ariostesca fortress in Castelnuovo di Garfagnana.

106__The Museum of Leprino
From the pastor to Pinocchio

Falerio Lepri, called Leprino, rebuilt the whole village of Santa Agata in miniature, including the pastor, the hairdresser, all the craftsmen, a pigpen, the village pub, and the school. He has also infused all the stories from the time when the now 93-year-old Leprino was a little boy into a landscape of cottages and villagers made out of papier-mâché. "The cobbler would always wear the shoes that people brought to him for repairs. Sundays at mass, one or another of the villagers would discover his shoes on the cobbler's feet," says Leprino. "When asked about the whereabouts of their shoes, he'd always give the same cheeky response: 'They're not ready yet.'"

The artist himself tells stories and anecdotes that you can hear recorded as you move from station to station, or better, from craft to craft. As of last year, there is also an English translation. The money for the multimedia addition was provided by EU development funds to support the recording of this special kind of history.

The 65 personalities in the miniature world of Santa Agata are neatly dressed in fabric and equipped with a small motor that can power the hand movements typical of their professions. Therefore, the museum is also called Vita Artigiana e Contadina con Personaggi in Movimento, or Rural and Artisan Life with Figures in Motion.

Leprino started this enterprise while still running the grocery store in the village, and when he retired, he decided to create the puppet museum. New figures are still being added to the collection today. There's already a Pinocchio.

For visitors, a trip to the museum is a delightful journey back in time to the rural society of the Mugello in the 1920s, when the village was poor, but the residents were relatively happy. "Drink more" reads the sign over the door to the village pub.

Address Centro Polivalente Sant'Agata (multipurpose building of the municipality of Santa Agata), Via Montaccianico 83a, 50038 Sant'Agata, Scarperia, Tel +39/055/8406750 or +39/055/8406750 | Getting there From Florence, head toward Borgo San Lorenzo. In San Piero a Sieve, continue in the direction of Scarperia until you reach Santa Agata. | Hours Sundays and holidays in summer 3:30–6:30pm, in winter 3–6pm. Call ahead in case it is closed. | Tip The nearby church of Santa Agata dates from the year 1000.

107__Il Fiore
The original Bistecca alla Fiorentina

In the best-case scenario, anyone ordering his *Bistecca alla Fiorentina* cooked well done can expect a scornful grin. More likely, the request will be flat-out denied. "You either eat your *bistecca* bloody or you don't eat it at all!" explains Leonardo Salvadori, the chef at the Ristorante Il Fiore, rather unyieldingly. The eatery has been known for decades throughout the region for the excellent quality of its steak.

They have served Tuscan specialties here since 1929, when grandparents ran a small grocery store with a *trattoria*. The old grocery store has now turned into a restaurant with a terrace. To this day, the *fiorentina* is the most famous dish served in the hills of the Florentine suburb.

The best T-bone steaks come from Chianina cattle, the largest breed of beef cattle in the world, which has its origins in the Chiana Valley, about 45 miles southeast of Florence. No slice of meat under four centimeters will be cut, and the steaks can be up to 2.5 inches thick. Thus a *bistecca* should weigh between 2.2 and 3.3 pounds. The meat is cut from the rear part of the back. The T-shaped bone and the roast beef with a filet mignon then make up the so-called Porterhouse or T-bone steak.

To prepare the steak perfectly, the grilling temperature and time must be precisely maintained, because the steak must be bloody and yet melt in your mouth at the same time. The meat develops its flavor while you chew it, so it must stay juicy. And this works only if the meat is practically raw on the inside. Were it actually well done, it would taste bitter at the end.

If someone still wants his meat to be pink, the chef recommends searing a piece of roast beef for a brief moment, or just ordering the filet. But, of course, then it would no longer be a true *Bistecca alla Fiorentina*.

Address Via di Marciola 112, 50018 Scandicci, Tel +39/055/768678 | Getting there
From Florence, it is about 8.5 miles to Scandicci on the SS 67, then take the SP 98 after
Marciola and follow the signs for Il Fiore. | Hours Daily 12:30–3:30pm and Thu–Sun
7:30–10:30pm | Tip Nearby, among the vineyards and olive groves, there are a number
of *agriturismi* such as Il Poderaccio (www.agriturismoilpoderaccio.it).

108___ The Hexagonal Tower
Masterful military architecture

The defiant hexagonal tower is widely visible from the A 11 Firenze-Mare highway, but most just speed right on past. It's worth a trip to the well-preserved medieval fortress complex, however. Here, on the slopes of Montalbano, at about the midpoint between the cities of Pistoia, Lucca, and Florence, there were seemingly endless violent military conflicts over the centuries.

The first of the city-states to rule Serravalle – which translates as something akin to "closing off the valley" – was Pistoia, which had already built the fortified walls and tower by the 12th century. In 1302, the Florentines and the Lucchese besieged Serravalle, shelled the fort, and starved the enemy for 89 days. Finally, Lucca took control. They immediately built new fortifications on the western side of the site and reinforced the existing walls with new ones on the eastern side.

The Rocca Vecchio, the older fortified tower that was also known as the Barbarossa Tower, has a square base and stands an impressive 131 feet high. The new tower, called the Castruccio Tower, is significantly taller and hexagonal – at that time a real military innovation. The tower was indeed perfectly suited as an observation post in the wide valley, but it was repeatedly altered in shape and structure to better accommodate the changing military requirements over the years.

The two towers stand very close to each other, and the guided tour provides visitors with a history of the development of defensive techniques. The complex still includes a cistern and a portion of the old walls in the Gabella gate, from which you can walk to the village of Gabella Vecchia, the old customs site located at the foot of the fortress. In the early evening, strollers come by to enjoy the tranquility of this once warlike place. From the top of the tower you can enjoy a panoramic view of the countryside.

Address 51030 Serravalle Pistoiese | Getting there Take the A11 to the Serravalle Pisoiese exit, then follow the signs for Rocca di Castriuccio. | Tip The view of the fortress from Castellina, a small town in the area, is especially good. In the summer, the town holds a medieval festival.

109___Oratorio della Madonna del Vannella

A Botticelli among 30 cypresses

If you turn onto the Via del Desiderio in Settignano, you'll catch an impressive sight on the corner: thirty cypress trees arranged in a semicircle with a view of the hilly landscape beyond. On this same corner stands a tiny church, which is usually closed. Centuries ago, the chapel was a tabernacle, a kind of house altar, just like those found by the hundreds on the street corners in Florence (see p. 128)

Even at that time, this place of piety kept guard over a rare gem: the fresco *Madonna and Child*, attributed to the famous artist Botticelli (though there are some who believe it to be a work of the artist Filippo Lippi). Legend has it that the Madonna appeared to the small Giovannella (called Vannella) while she was tending her sheep in the village. The tabernacle with the Madonna was dedicated to the miracle.

The Congregazione del trentesimo (Congregation of the thirtieth), one of the oldest organizations in the town of Settignano was responsible for the tabernacle and the 15th-century Madonna. They named themselves after the thirty cypresses, which corresponded to the number of members in the organization. They soon had the tabernacle converted into a chapel in order to protect the fresco from the harsh environmental conditions. The men of the congregation still take care of the chapel today (only the paternal leader of a family can join), and those who would like to visit must contact the chairman.

Settignano has always been a home to artists, and many visit the town because of the church, which plays host to the occasional art exhibition. Maybe it is the somewhat blurred appearance of the Madonna – and the cypress grove, of course – that give the chapel its special atmosphere.

Address Via D. da Settignano 56b, 50135 Settignano, www.oratoriovannella.it, guidodegli@tiscali.it | Getting there From Florence, about six miles via Piazza della Libertà, Piazza delle Cure, Viale delle Mille, through Coverciano (soccer stadium) in the direction of Settignano. Upon arriving at the piazza on Via S. Romano, turn left onto Via Desiderio da Settignano, and after about a half mile, you'll see the small cypress grove. | Hours To visit, make a request by email a few days prior. | Tip The Casa del Popolo on the piazza in Settignano offers aperitifs at reasonable prices, with a great view out into the hilly green landscape.

110__ The Road of the 92nd Battalion

The sacrifice of John Fox

Every year, on December 26, a band from the town of Barga comes and plays *Fratelli d'Italia*, the Italian national anthem, in front of the village church. The community of 142 souls commemorates the tragedy that happened here more than 70 years ago, and the mayor gives a speech, often accompanied by an icy wind that blows during this time of year in the mountains of Garfagnana, north of Lucca.

At four o'clock in the morning on December 26, 1944, 29-year-old John Fox, who was sitting at his observation post in the tower, was awoken with a start by shelling. As the sun rose, the American lieutenant saw that the village was completely surrounded by German troops. Fox gave the command to his countrymen to fire on his own position. He shouted, "Shoot! There are many more of them than there are of us!" The ratio was one to eight for the German Wehrmacht. After three days, the Americans had retaken the tower and found Fox's body under the rubble with about 70 German soldiers who had been shot by American soldiers – just like John Fox.

Fox was part of the 92nd Battalion, known as the Buffalo Soldiers, a segregated unit made up entirely of African Americans. Their task was to push back the German forces to the so-called Gothic Line. The Gothic Line was a 320-kilometer-long defensive position that divided the Italian peninsula in half after the Allied landings in Sicily in 1943: in the north were the Germans, and the Allies controlled everything to the south.

The film *Miracle at Santa Anna* (2008), directed by Spike Lee, tells the story of the 92nd Battalion and this little-known chapter of World War II. Some of the scenes were filmed on Monte Lama in Sommocolonia.

Address Via del 92. Divisione "Buffalo," 55051 Sommocolonia | **Getting there**
From Barga, take the SP7 toward Castelvecchio Pascoli for about a mile; in Ponte di
Catagana, at the Corsonna River, turn right and follow the signs for Sommocolonia
(about 3.75 miles). | Tip The small museum displays memorabilia from World War II.
Visits are by request (email cultura@comunedibarga.it).

111 __ The Prison in the Palazzo Pretorio

Five centuries of graffiti

Some people will certainly find fault with their grammatical failings and their artistic value, but the writings and drawings on the walls of the prison in the Palazzo Pretorio impressively document the life, love, and sorrow of its inmates. Until 1923, all kinds of prisoners served out their sentences here, from the petty chicken thief from Livorno, who sat in the same dark cell on three occasions between 1898 and 1919 ("3 volte qua dentro"), to political prisoners and soldiers who had broken ranks during the time of the fascists.

The medieval fortress in Vicopisano was designed in 1438 by the Master Filippo Brunelleschi, the architect famous for the dome on the Duomo in Florence. Just a few years ago, the walls of the prison cells were restored at great cost, and several layers of wall paintings expressing the prisoners' exclamations of anger and despair came to light. Thousands of pieces of graffiti are emblazoned there, telling the history of Italy from a unique perspective, some dating from as far back as the late 16th century.

The ground floor of the fortress was set aside for common criminals who only served short sentences. It is not difficult to imagine the desperation in the dark cells, some of which have neither windows nor toilets.

There were both public and secret prisons as far back as the Middle Ages, and this dichotomy persisted for many centuries. Here, the cells used by the secret police, or *le segrete*, are on the upper floors. In general, political rebels from the area were usually locked up here. Prisoners stayed longer in these cells, and the hygienic conditions were somewhat better. Symbols like the hammer and sickle and anti-fascist slogans made by the prisoners appear right alongside the fascist "Death to spies of the secret police!"

Address Palazzo Pretorio, Via Del Pretorio 1, 56010 Vicopisano | **Getting there** From Pisa take the SS Pisa-Firenze to the Cascina exit, and follow signs along the provincial road for Vicopisano. | **Hours** Sat 3:30–7:30pm, Sun 10am–12:30pm, 3:30–7:30pm | **Tip** Local delicacies are served at the Osteria di Ceppato (Tue–Sun 12:30–2pm and 7:30–10pm, www.osteriadiceppato.com).

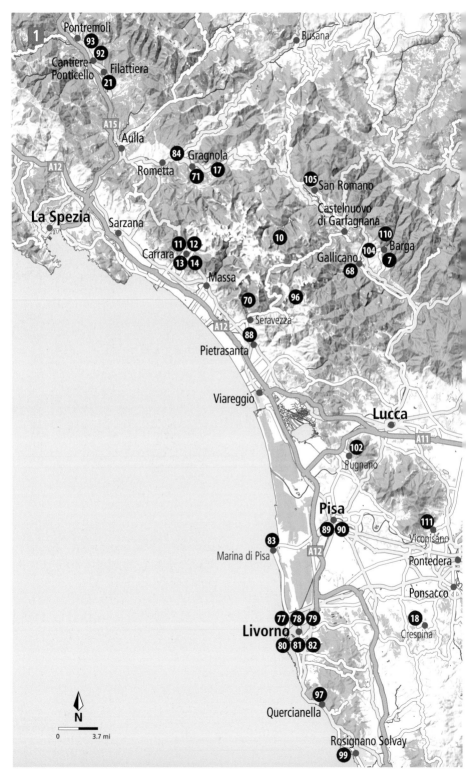

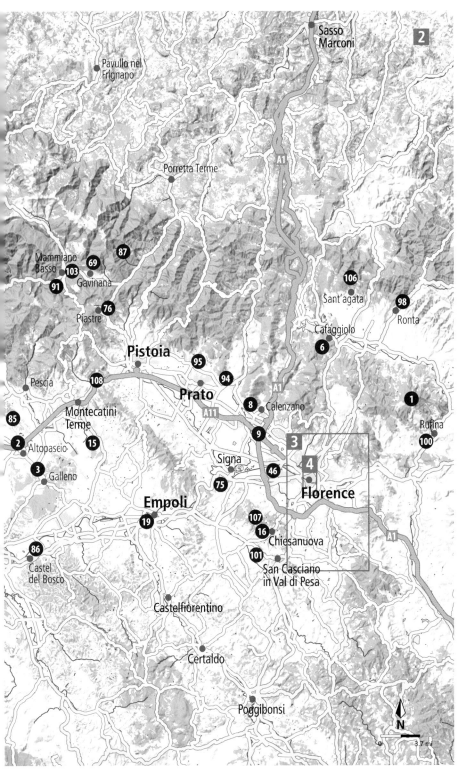

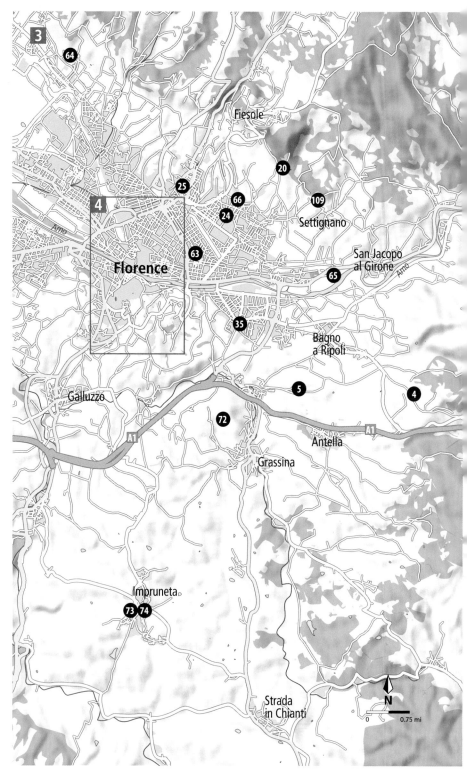

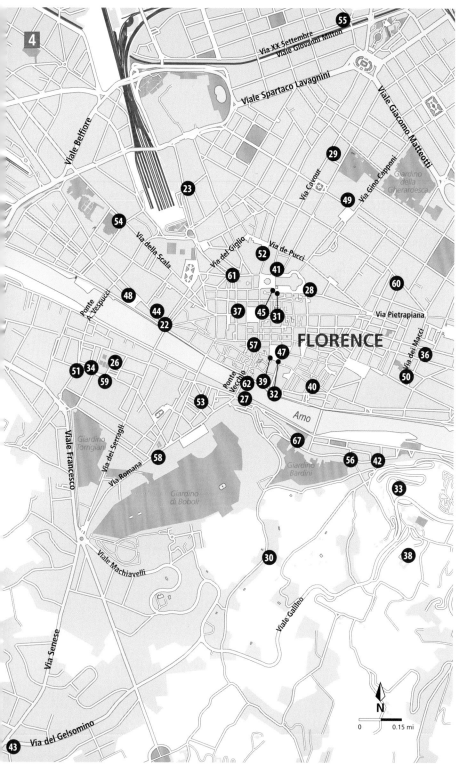

Lucia Jay von Seldeneck,
Carolin Huder, Verena Eidel
**111 PLACES IN BERLIN
THAT YOU SHOULDN'T MISS**
ISBN 978-3-95451-208-9

Rüdiger Liedtke
**111 PLACES IN MUNICH
THAT YOU SHOULDN'T MISS**
ISBN 978-3-95451-222-5

Rike Wolf
**111 PLACES IN HAMBURG
THAT YOU SHOULDN'T MISS**
ISBN 978-3-95451-234-8

Paul Kohl
**111 PLACES IN BERLIN
ON THE TRAIL OF THE NAZIS**
ISBN 978-3-95451-323-9

John Sykes
**111 PLACES IN LONDON
THAT YOU SHOULDN'T MISS**
ISBN 978-3-95451-346-8

Dirk Engelhardt
**111 PLACES IN BARCELONA
THAT YOU MUST NOT MISS**
ISBN 978-3-95451-353-6

Peter Eickhoff
**111 PLACES IN VIENNA
THAT YOU SHOULDN'T MISS**
ISBN 978-3-95451-206-5

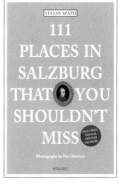

Stefan Spath
**111 PLACES IN SALZBURG
THAT YOU SHOULDN'T MISS**
ISBN 978-3-95451-230-0

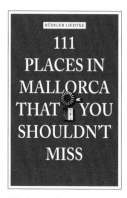

Rüdiger Liedtke
**111 PLACES ON MALLORCA
THAT YOU SHOULDN'T MISS**
ISBN 978-3-95451-281-2

Marcus X. Schmid
**111 PLACES IN ISTANBUL
THAT YOU MUST NOT MISS**
ISBN 978-3-95451-423-6

Ralf Nestmeyer
**111 PLACES IN PROVENCE
THAT YOU MUST NOT MISS**
ISBN 978-3-95451-422-9

Christiane Bröcker,
Babette Schröder
**111 PLACES IN STOCKHOLM
THAT YOU MUST NOT MISS**
ISBN 978-3-95451-459-5

Gerd Wolfgang Sievers
**111 PLACES IN VENICE
THAT YOU MUST NOT MISS**
ISBN 978-3-95451-460-1

Petra Sophia Zimmermann
**111 PLACES IN VERONA
AND LAKE GARDA THAT
YOU MUST NOT MISS**
ISBN 978-3-95451-611-7

Annett Klingner
**111 PLACES IN ROME
THAT YOU MUST NOT MISS**
ISBN 978-3-95451-469-4

Jo-Anne Elikann
**111 PLACES IN NEW YORK
THAT YOU MUST NOT MISS**
ISBN 978-3-95451-052-8

All photos © Francesco P. Carbone, except: Chapters 15, 23, 32, 33, 56, 57, 64, 69, 86, 91, 92, 99, 107 Beate C. Kirchner; Chapter 21 Naturalmente Lunigiana; Chapter 26 The Art Archive Ref. AA344931; Chapter 49 ICM no. 6798 from September 5, 2014; Chapter 70 Azienda Agricola Lorenzoni; Chapter 79 Dario Antichi; Chapter 97 Silvana Malevolti (top), Natalie Kirchner (bottom); Chapter 101 Azienda Agricola Villa Montepaldi

Many thanks to:
Alessandro Bargagna and Chiara Celli, City Grand Tour, Pisa; Paolo Belardinelli, Accademia della Crusca; Monica Berti, Florence; Luigi Boni, AC Firenze; Beppe Bracaloni, Vicopisano; Conte Niccolò Capponi, Florence; Mariassunta Casaroli, Province of Lucca; Viola Di Lembo, Venturina; Marco Donati, Florence; Don Bernardo, San Miniato al Monte; Fabio Feri, Alessandra Ambruosi and Martina, Florence; Sabina Feroci, Marcello Cucurnia and Margherita, Marina di Carrara; Community Library San Marcello Pistoiese; Simone Guaita, Florence; Dott. Giuseppe Guanci, Prato; Flavio Guidi, Barga; Massimo Innocenti, Scarperia; Natalie Kirchner, Munich; Silvana Malevolti, Quercianella; Roberto Masi, Pontasieve; Vanessa Montigiani and Dott.ssa Ilaria Di Fidio, Sigma CSC, Florence; Giovanni Orlandini, Florence; Marco Rossi and Martina Guerrini, Livorno; Dott.ssa Gisa Rubino, Florence; Dott. Rubino, Vicopisano; Roberta, Community Library Altopascio; Roberta Tucci, Commune of Bagno a Ripoli; Francesco Serena, Florence; Simona, Visitlunigiana; Paolo Vignaroli and Alessandra, Florence; Renate Wolf, Munich; and Sauro Zei, Impruneta, to whom chapter 74 is dedicated.

The Author

Beate C. Kirchner was born in 1960 in Munich and studied in Florence and Munich. After attaining her degree in political science, she worked for many years as a manager for German magazines. Today she is an independent journalist and author in the fields of business, politics, and travel. She visits Florence and Tuscany several times a year.

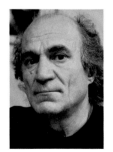

The Photographer

Francesco P. Carbone, born in 1960 in Calabria, has lived in Tuscany for over 30 years. There he began his career as a photographer, focusing on social themes, people, and culture. He has traveled in Italy as a photojournalist (for example "The Marble Workers in Carrara" and "Waiting Rooms in Italy") and throughout the world, including in Cuba and Spain ("The Roma in the Nazareth Neighborhood of Valencia"), among others. He and his camera are on the hunt for further images that awaken the emotions.